EVERYTHING I KNOW ABOUT THE MUSIC BUSINESS
I LEARNED FROM
MY COUSIN RICK

The musician's practical guide to success

by Dave Rose

Library Classification-in-publishing information:

Published by Shuman & Goldstein Publishing Co., LTD.,
White Plains, New York/Raleigh, North Carolina

Manufactured in the United States of America

www.DaveRose.info

www.MyCousinRick.com

www.ShumanAndGoldstein.com

Book designed by Madeline Newberry, Melodie Moorefield-Wilson and Carter Peery

Special thanks to Carter Perry, John Booker, Elizabeth Barrett, Melodie Moorefield-Wilson, Madeline Newberry, Hannah Parker, Callie Rivers, Allison Moorer, Melanie Long, Jeff Holshouser, Taylor Bureau, and Charles Marshall

Rose, Dave.

Everything I Know About the Music Business I Learned from My Cousin Rick/ Dave Rose – 1st. ed.

p.cm.

ISBN-10 0615703666
ISBN-13 9780615703664

10 9 8 7 6 5

Author's Note

I wrote this book based primarily on my personal experiences and observations in the music business during the last twenty-five years. I also drew heavily from my archives and memorabilia -- as evidenced by the old photographs spread throughout the book. All of the photographs are part of my personal collection. They were either taken by me, or in a few instances, by my longtime business partner and friend, Andy Martin. In some cases, I may not have recalled a specific conversation *exactly* as it occurred, word-for-word, but I have recalled or re-created the substance of the conversations and events as accurately as possible based on my personal first-hand observations, recollections, and archives. The purpose behind the stories in this book is to help musicians learn how to advance their career by studying those who have achieved success.

Special thanks are in order for each and every one of the artists mentioned throughout this book that I have had the pleasure to work with, represent, or even just meet during these years. Each one of them has been instrumental to my development in the music business and to the lessons I've tried to impart, in my own way, throughout this book. On that note, very special thanks goes to my cousin Rick, who served as the obvious inspiration for this book by kick starting my continual quest to find more brilliant music.

This book is dedicated to:

My English teacher who said,
"Dave, writing just isn't your thing."

My music teacher who said,
"Dave, music just isn't your thing."

My ex-girlfriend who said,
"Dave, you need to give up on this music business dream and get a real job."

And to my parents, Joe and Ruth Rose, who remained supportive by always giving me unconditional love despite surely knowing there were elements of truth in what all of these people said.

My loving parents
Thanks Mom and Dad!

"All bands fart and argue. It's just part of the
creative process."

-Matt Thomas, *Parmalee*

EVERYTHING I KNOW ABOUT THE MUSIC BUSINESS I LEARNED FROM MY COUSIN RICK

The musician's practical guide to success

Contents

Chapter 4: All About Recording

Chapter 5: Booking, Venues, and Touring

Chapter 6: What's Next?

Foreword

by Allison Moorer

Music and business have always been strange bedfellows. They are polar opposites at their essences. Music, a soul redeeming art form at its best, is born of emotion and inspiration, then expressed to find unity and shared experience with the world and other beings, as all art forms are. Business is about commerce; about gaining monetary advantage over others.

So how do the two go together? Well, they don't really. It's an age-old struggle and oft-debated question that we've been batting around for years and isn't likely ever to be solved. And Lord knows I'm not going to try here. But let it be said that the two sides need each other. Without artists, the business people would have nothing to sell, and without the business people, we artists would likely starve. It's not a match made in heaven, but it is possible that the two worlds can come together to great effect. When that happens everyone wins. But it is hardly ever an accident. What goes on behind the scenes is mind-blowing.

Anyone can make music for themselves and some people are happy to just play in their living rooms for fun and never worry about taking it further than that. Good for them. They'll probably have more stable lives and less heartbreak. But if you want to be a person who makes their living, either partially or wholly, from playing music, there are certain realities that must be faced. No one is going to come knock on your door and discover you. It takes hard work and determination to get out, get seen, and get anywhere.

And that's what Dave discusses, in great detail and very well, between these covers. He's not telling you how to write songs or sing them (only to do both well), but sorting out the steps to take after you've begun to figure that part out for yourself (you'll never figure it out completely, that's part of being an artist). I remember telling a young songwriter once when asked for advice, "Work on your craft. Write as much as you can stand to. Listen to and study other writers that you like. If you don't work on your craft as a songwriter, you won't know what to do with an idea when it comes to you." My husband says it is like catching lightning in a bottle. So you better have a bottle handy.

There is no proven formula for success. There are plenty of musicians and bands out there who do everything right. They have a Facebook page with a lot of likes, they tweet constantly, have a great website, they have pro gear, they play gigs with decent turnouts, they have a record produced by a brand-name producer, and they still can't get noticed by the industry heavyweights. Who knows why they don't connect? Could be the songs, could be a lack of star quality, could be not being in the right place at the right time. But really, no one can honestly put a finger on why some things work in the marketplace and some things don't. If this were possible, then there would be more successes and fewer failures.

Having said that, I'd bet that if a record label had their eye on two bands whose music they liked equally, and one had their stuff together and one didn't, they'd sign the one that had it together. The truth is, sometimes it comes down to luck. But luck won't do you any good if you don't put yourself in a position to be lucky by laying a proper foundation. So do that, as Dave says, then write and sing and play your butt off.

Chapter 1:
The Pursuit of Success

The root of the successful musician

In the '60s and '70s bands used to say, "If I could just get the phone number to the big A&R rep[1] at the record label, I could call him and let him know about our band. He would sign us and all our worries would be over."

Then in the '80s, publications and magazines flooded the marketplace with this very information. The phone numbers and addresses for every major label and their staff were at your fingertips. Bands were now able to call these A&R reps and even mail them their demos. Yet, somehow, things didn't change. So bands started saying, "If I could just get the A&R rep to come out and hear my band live, all of our worries would be over."

In the '90s, there was a trend to sign bands that already had somewhat of a regional following. Thus, bands hopped in their vans and toured relentlessly in hopes of gaining that regional following so they could take those industry publications from the '80s and call A&R reps with news of their growing fan base.

Yet, nothing really changed.

As the '90s came to a close (and particularly in the mid-2000s), we entered the Internet age and music was more accessible than ever. With one click, you could find out everything you wanted to know about the record label you've been hoping would sign you. You could email them, become their friend on Facebook, and communicate with them via Twitter. Labels started finding bands on the Internet and bands said, "If I could just get enough friends on

---

[1] A&R Rep: *Artists and Repertoire Representative*. Label talent scout and artist development.

Facebook, or enough followers on Twitter, or enough hits on YouTube, all of my worries would be over."

But they weren't.

Bands felt that if they could just start a conversation with the A&R rep, or if they could just get the A&R rep out to hear them, or if they could just capture their attention on the Internet, their worries would be over. Bands focused on getting the A&R rep's attention more than they focused on *what* would get their attention: brilliant songs combined with amazing musicianship, suitable image, and a real fan base (not some number counter on a website; I mean real, true, passionate fans).

The problem has never been the lack of a phone number, contact information, or email address. The problem was that bands were focused on the wrong thing.

This book is designed to get to the root of what makes a band or musician successful. It teaches you how to learn and navigate through the business of music.

This book will not give you phone numbers, a magic website, or that secret thing to say to an A&R rep. Even if you had that information, the road to success is far from guaranteed.

What I can do is this: show you how to make your band a *great* band. A *desirable* band. A band that makes *your* phone ring with interest from others. This book will give you the basic fundamentals that all successful bands have proven to work. This book will teach you what matters and what doesn't. And whether it's the year 1975 or 2035, the same principals will apply.

How do I know this? The same principals have applied since the beginning of music: brilliant music combined with a rock-solid work ethic will ensure a path to success.

Who am I to give you advice?

I'm a guy who loves music and has loved playing it ever since my college friend taught me the D, C, and G chords on a guitar. I'm a guy who has played in bands, some good, some not so good. I've slept in the back of a van because I couldn't afford a hotel. I've opened my guitar case on the streets and played for spare change just to get enough gas money to go to the next town. I've played at some of the best and worst dive bars in the nation. I have been the epitome of the struggling and starving musician.

And yet I've also managed the careers of Grammy-winning and Billboard-charting artists. I have an office lined with gold and platinum records. I've had the joy of meeting and working with some of the biggest names in the entertainment business.

Most importantly, what I think qualifies me to give you advice is that I'm a guy who has, at one time or another, made almost every single possible mistake you can make in the music business. But I learned from them.

The marriage of art and commerce has always interested me, mostly because the two seemingly have nothing in common. Art is creative and free, while commerce is numerical and structured. The ability to bring the two together fascinates me.

The first band I played in was an '80s hair band around the time of cassette tapes. We went into a local recording studio and recorded four songs. I researched where to get those tapes duplicated and we had 100 printed up. It was my first "real" release.

I recall the first show we played after releasing that tape. I went back to the merchandise table after the show, mostly to meet girls. We had a crowd of 30 or so people waiting in the lobby when we came out. As soon as I jumped behind our merchandise table and pulled out a box of cassettes, I instantly had someone hand me $5 and say, "I'll take one. You guys sounded good."

POW! It hit me. That moment changed my life. You mean I can create a song in my brain, record that song, and people will pay

Embarrassing picture #1 of many. My first band – Majesty ("The cassette tape era"). That's me with the "thumbs up."

money for it? You have got to be kidding me. Sign me up. This is awesome.

I was one of the rare musicians who was as fascinated with the business of music as I was with the music itself.

I made every mistake known to mankind during my first years as a musician. If there was a mistake a band could make, I made it. But I did my best to learn from, and not repeat, those mistakes.

In 1995, I went on to start Deep South Records with my college buddy, Andy Martin. We put out some compilation CDs and a few other titles. We ended up doing pretty well, releasing songs by **Marcy Playground, Five for Fighting, Butch Walker, Sister Hazel, SR-71**, and a dozen or so more that would go on to achieve some level of international notoriety.

At an early stage in my career, I realized I had a gift for picking out good talent. I don't say that pretentiously, it just came very naturally to me. To me, it was as clear as day when a band or artist had *it*: that intangible but undeniable element that made them special.

After releasing some records successfully, we added a management arm to our company. In the years that followed, we managed some of the greatest artists in the business, including **Little Feat, Bruce Hornsby, Stryper, Parmalee, Allison Moorer, SR-71, Marcy Playground, Vienna Teng, Lee Roy Parnell, The Warren Brothers, Jason Michael Carroll,** and many more.

Around the mid-2000s, we added a concert and event production division to our company, producing some of the largest events in the Carolinas. Then, in 2007, I opened a small live music venue in Raleigh, North Carolina.

I did, and still do, work in almost every aspect of the music business and have thus had the opportunity to screw up about anything that can possibly be screwed up. I'm just a guy who took those screw-ups, figured out where I went wrong and used those lessons to better the careers of some of the most highly respected artists in the industry.

I don't feel like I've worked a day in my life because I love what I do. Long before I knew you could make money in the business, I loved it. And I'd be doing it with or without the money. Music is in my blood. If it's in yours too, I can help you avoid some of the mistakes I made along the way.

Me and Andy Martin

I'm here to help. Let's get started.

Just by deciding to try to "make it" in music, you have decided to enter a profession where the vast majority of people who enter this field never make a living. I can't think of any other career where it is so rare for people to succeed, even if they do everything by the book. Go to medical school and you will very likely become a doctor. Go to law school and you will very likely become a lawyer. But chances are, if you enter the field of music as your career choice, it's highly unlikely you will become a professional musician.

I don't say that to discourage you. I say it because you need to know that this is an extremely competitive and complex field. I mean, who wouldn't want to be a rock star? It sounds great, but it requires work, discipline, and a unique creative element that is deeply rooted in your heart and soul. My guess is that you already have the creative element, or are at least heading in that direction. It's the other stuff that is the hard part.

The basic concepts of getting your music heard by the masses are timeless. Although we'll touch on some of today's technology that can help advance your career, I won't be giving you a list of the latest and greatest websites or recording technology that will catapult you into stardom—because frankly, there is no such thing. You can utilize technology, the Internet, and social media to expand your audience, but without great music, it doesn't really matter how much you may know about new innovations in the industry.

Meet Cousin Rick

Flashback to 1977: I was on a family vacation in Holden Beach, North Carolina. My older cousin, Rick, was the coolest guy in the world to me. He had long hair. He surfed. He knew all the pretty girls. And he loved rock-n-roll. I always looked up to him.

One afternoon, he showed me his new stereo, which had the latest and greatest turntable. He pulled out an album and said to me, "Have you heard this band, BOSTON?"

Trying to be cool I said, "Yeah, man. I have." Although in reality, at this point in my life, my musical horizons had not extended much beyond the 45's I purchased with my allowance, which consisted primarily of songs I had heard on Top 40 radio.

He put on the album and cranked up his new hi-fidelity stereo and there it was: BOSTON's first album. My world would change forever from that point. That was the first time I even realized that bands put out full albums. It was also the first time I realized that an entire album could be great. All I knew were songs on the radio and I barely knew the artists who sang those songs.

My cousin Rick went on and on telling me all about BOSTON. The history of the band and everything he knew about them and their album. He made sure to point out particularly great parts throughout the recording. I held the cover while reading the liner notes and soaking up everything I could possibly absorb.

"This is some cool stuff, huh?" he said.

"Yeah, man. I love it."

I saved my allowance and later the next week my friend and I both went out and bought our own copies of BOSTON's first album.

It was the first full album I had ever purchased. My second was the Kiss *Alive* album, although that one had been out for a few years by the time I purchased it.

Had it been today, my cousin Rick would have emailed me a YouTube link to a BOSTON song. I would have watched it, loved it, and emailed it to several other friends. A few of my friends would probably purchase a few songs, or maybe even the entire album.

My cousin Rick and I in Holden Beach, NC

One of my friends would probably tweet about it, and another would post a link on Facebook.

When cousin Rick first introduced me to BOSTON, it was about a two-week process between the time he played me the album and when I bought a copy of my own.

Today, the process would have taken a few minutes, tops.

But the underlying point is the same. BOSTON made great music. Undeniably great music. Music that was so unique and creative that when someone heard it, they *had* to tell someone else about it.

I imagine when Tom Scholz (founder of BOSTON) was making that record, he wasn't concerned with all the different ways to get the music heard. It was his first record. He cared about making the best album possible. He cared about creating songs that were undeniably great. Timeless songs. And he probably knew that if he made a truly great album, the rest would somehow take care of itself. And it did.

In today's technological world, it's easy to lose focus of the one goal that is really most important: to make great music. You won't get it right your first time, or even your second time, but keep at it and you'll get it right.

Make great music and people will tell other people. Maybe it's by playing an album on a turntable in 1977, or maybe it's by emailing a YouTube clip today, but if you make truly great music, people will pass it on. Looking back on it, my cousin Rick unknowingly taught me that great music will find a way to be heard.

Me, Michael Sweet, and Tom Scholz

What do you want?

"We wanna be successful. We wanna be successful in music. Ya know what I mean?"

About a year ago a very persistent local band called and emailed me almost daily wanting to line up a meeting with me. When we finally met I asked them, "So, what exactly is it that you want to do?" That was their answer. And the conversation continued like this:

<u>Me</u>: *Actually, no. I don't know what you mean. What do you mean by successful?*

<u>Band</u>: *You know. We wanna be successful. We wanna make a living playing music.*

<u>Me</u>: *That's it? That's easy. I can have you doing that within 30 days.*

Their faces lit up as if they had just won the lottery.

<u>Band</u>: *I knew we came to the right place. Cool.* (I believe there was even

a high-five or two exchanged among the members at that point).

Me: *Alrighty, here's what we're gonna do. You need to get yourself some nice suits. Learn a bunch of Top 40 and dance songs and we'll get you playing the wedding and corporate circuit.*

Looks of confusion and disappointment passed from one member to the next.

Band: *No, no, no…. I mean we wanna make a living playing OUR music. Music that WE write.*

Me: *Okay. Not quite as easy, but we can take care of that. There are dozens and dozens of what I call menu-venues within a hundred mile radius. You'd play acoustic normally, often over the dinner crowd. You'd be stuck in a back corner somewhere and nobody would really be paying attention, but those places pay pretty well. You won't get rich, but you can definitely make a living playing sports bars and menu-venues, playing your own music.*

Thoroughly disappointed at this point, they took some time to think before spitting out their rebuttal.

Band: *Okay. Okay. We got it. Here's what we want. We want to be on the radio.*

After a brief pause, another band member spoke up to continue that sentence "…. on the radio with OUR music that WE write."

Me: *Gotcha. No problem. I can have you on the radio, with your music, by this afternoon. There are literally thousands of Internet radio stations that will play almost anything. You upload your song to those stations and before the end of the day, I'd bet dozens of them will have played it. Not too many people listen to some of the smaller Internet radio stations, but you will have been successful. Your music, your songs, on the radio.*

Band: *No. That's not what we meant at all. We want to be on the real radio, like Big Rock 103.7.*

At this point, another band member chimes in, "Yeah, I love that station. They just played the new Kings of Leon today."

Band: *Yeah, we want to be played on THAT radio station (pause)… playing our music. Music that we write.*

Me: *Again, not a problem. I can have you on Big Rock 103.7 by the end of the week. On Sunday nights at 11pm they have a Local Band show from 11pm to Midnight. The DJ is a friend of mine. I can get you played on that show and THEN you will have been successful.*

One of the band members smiled sheepishly and said, "*I see what you're doing. You're trying to confuse us.*"

Me: *Quite the contrary. You're <u>already</u> confused. You came in here expecting me to make you successful when you yourself have not even defined what success is. Go back to your practice room and talk about that, and let's meet again in a month.*

But really think it through. Think about it in extreme detail, because when we meet up a month from now, I'm going to ask you the same question I asked when we started this conversation: What exactly is it you want to do? Just knowing the answer to that question is going to get you started in the right direction, and then maybe I can help.

This is a problem for the vast majority of local bands. They never define success. They never define what exactly it is they want. And how can you achieve something when you don't know what it is you're trying to achieve?

> *Cousin Rick says:* Define success, specifically by writing five short-term and long-term goals. Hang this list in a place you will see it every day.

Ryan Adams

It's a requirement that anyone from Raleigh tell you their Ryan Adams story. In the southeast, it's similar to anyone from Columbia, South Carolina being required to tell you a Hootie & The Blowfish story, or people from Athens, Georgia being required to share a B-

23

52s, REM, or Widespread Panic story. Those from Raleigh are required to share their Ryan Adams story. Here's mine, and how it relates to the music business.

In 1995, as I was starting Deep South Records, I was also the bass player in 9811 (Ninety-Eight Eleven). We were recording our first album in a studio called The Funny Farm in Apex, North Carolina with the studio owner and engineer, Greg Woods. 9811 was recording at the same time Whiskeytown was recording, in the same studio. Whiskeytown was Ryan Adams' first band. 9811 would record for a few days and then Whiskeytown would come in for a few days. One morning we arrived and Greg said to me, "Man, you have *got* to hear this shit I recorded last night." He proceeded to play me "Matrimony" and "Hard Luck Story," which ended up on the first Whiskeytown album. He couldn't stop talking about it, how great it was, and the magic of these amazing songs.

We spent the first couple hours of 9811's session listening to stuff he had recorded with Whiskeytown the night before. And I've got to admit, I was blown away. Incredible. It was the first time I had heard them. And I'm honored to this day to have had the opportunity to hear Ryan Adams music long before the rest of the world did, not to mention be a musician recording in the same studio as him, with the same engineer.

But in hindsight, I should have realized exactly what was going on here. Greg wasn't playing *my* songs for Ryan Adams when *he* came in to record. No. Greg was playing Ryan's songs for me. Greg would light up like a glowing Christmas tree and cut into 9811's recording time just to play me stuff he had recorded with Ryan the night before.

Don't get me wrong. I loved it. It was my kind of music. And I couldn't get enough. Every time he'd play me something, I'd ask to hear more. But I wasn't savvy enough in the music business to realize what was going on.

Remember, when you make great music, undeniably great music, your cousin Rick will tell people about it. Or in this case, your engineer, Greg. Ryan Adams was making undeniably great music. I wasn't. My recordings were filed under the category of "pay the rent" for that studio.

When you are making your own recordings, are people going out of their way -- *way* out of their way -- to tell other people about it? If not, re-think things. And figure out why. It's not to say that everyone's first recording should have the effect that Ryan Adam's first recording did. It's only to say that you should be mindful and cognizant of the effect your music is having on people, or in my case, the lack thereof. Very few people get it right the first time. So don't avoid recording just because you think it may not be perfect. It takes time. Just be mindful of the reaction you're getting, and don't ignore it like I did.

Knowing now what I didn't know then, I should have realized: Okay, Ryan Adams = Brilliant. Dave Rose = Eh, not so much.

But I was just doing the best I could, learning as I went along. That's the fun of the music business: the journey. I was just making the best possible record I could, all the while entering my morning recording sessions only to have the incredible opportunity to listen to one of the greatest songwriters of our generation, and what he had recorded the night before.

It gives me chills to think I recorded in the same studio as Ryan Adams.

I wasn't a complete idiot though. The next year at the South by Southwest music conference, there was a thing called The Mentor Session. In these sessions, various industry professionals would offer 5 minutes of their time to "coach" aspiring musicians. You could read through the list of industry pros in advance and sign up for who you'd like to meet with for 5 minutes. There were some *huge* industry names in these sessions, and as a result it was hard to get a slot with some of the "big names". So I signed up to meet with an unknown name to most, an executive from the record label that Whiskeytown was signed to. It was that year at South by Southwest that really catapulted Whiskeytown into the media spotlight.

I spent 5 minutes with a record executive for a relatively unknown artist at the time. I wanted to find out what he knew. How did he know this was going to be big? What nuggets of music business information could I get from this genius that had our recording engineer spending most of his time playing us music from the band he had recorded the night before?

I spent the beginning of my 5 minutes with the Record Company Guy telling him my limited history in the studio with Whiskeytown. I was one of the very first people to hear Whiskeytown's recordings because our bands had recorded at the same studio around the same time. After hearing their music, I knew in my gut that this was the most brilliant music I had ever heard. From this I learned how it is important to trust your instincts.

Yet, still being the young kid I was, I needed to ask Mr. Record Company Guy, "What made you want to sign Whiskeytown?"

With a nice smile he said, "You heard the same music I did. Isn't it obvious? It's great music."

He did proceed to tell me about some of the marketing tactics they were using to promote Whiskeytown, which I enjoyed and soaked up, but I was mostly interested in how Whiskeytown got discovered.

You see, I still had not learned that it's all about the music. Make brilliant music, and the industry will find you. Instead, I thought Ryan Adams must have had some secret phone number to contact Mr. Record Company Guy. Instead, I thought Ryan Adams must have had a team of skilled publicists who carefully crafted a buzz that ultimately got Whiskeytown noticed. I thought Ryan Adams surely had a mailing list the size of Texas and had been sending out music to every known heartbeat in the industry. Nope. Ryan made brilliant music. People heard it and just had to tell someone else.

You couldn't *not* tell someone when you heard that music.

And when you find that music which is spreading like a wild fire, ask questions to those who are involved. Learn all that you can.

Don't think you have all the answers. You don't. When you hear your cousin Rick or your engineer Greg telling you about music, and you see the spark in their soul when they share this music with you, find out everything you can about that music. What makes it connect? What marketing strategies are being used to connect it with the masses? How did this music come to fruition? Learn anything and everything you can about the great artists you are being told about.

There's a reason people are telling people about that music. Find out why. Anything at all that you can find out, and it will put you one step further along on your career path.

I work with Caitlin Cary now, who was the "other half" of Whiskeytown with Ryan Adams, and she's still turning out undeniably brilliant music. Research her bands The Small Ponds and Tres Chicas.

When Ryan Adams makes music, your cousin Rick is sure to tell you about it. Create music that will have that same effect and you're heading down the path of a career in music.

> *Cousin Rick says:* Make a list of three bands or artists whom you first discovered because a friend told you about them.

For the love of music.

A notable actor once had a fan say to him, "I'd love to trade places with you. I'd love to be rich and famous."

The actor responded to the fan by saying, "Try being rich first. See if that doesn't solve most of your problems. The fame part really isn't all it's cracked up to be."

It's funny how those two words, "rich" and "famous", are frequently used together, and usually interchangeably. In reality, the two are often completely unrelated.

If you're getting into music either to be rich or to be famous, you're likely in it for the wrong reasons. You have to love music, pure and simple. Not to mention, you've chosen probably the most difficult path to lead you to either of these destinations. The vast majority of musicians get neither rich *nor* famous.

There are plenty of ways to do both without music.

But if you *do* have a love for music, and you *have* decided this is what you want to do, then be sure to recognize the vast difference between those two words, rich and famous. I know many rich musicians that are relatively unknown by the mainstream public. And I know many famous musicians who are broke, not because they squandered their millions, they just haven't made that much money.

Let's assume you love music. It's in your blood and this is what you're going to do. Do you want to be rich? On the other hand, do you want to be famous? Because very few professional musicians are both.

If you want to be famous, audition for a reality TV show. You won't make much money, but you'll be known by many. If you want to be rich, try your hand at some alternative career paths in music, maybe songwriting, producing records, or music publishing. The really rich people I know in music are almost *un*known by the rest of the world. Many are songwriters. Some are producers. Some get into music publishing or some other form of music business. Many of the unknown rich musicians are multi-millionaires, far wealthier than the famous artists who have recorded the unknown rich musicians' songs. A songwriter can even walk into a grocery store on a Saturday afternoon and not a single person would know who he is.

Butch Walker (second from the left) used to stay at my house when touring through Raleigh. He's a brilliant artist, but made his money writing songs and producing for some of the biggest names in the business: Avril Lavigne, Katy Perry, Panic at the Disco, Pink, Weezer, and more.

> *Cousin Rick says:* If you had to choose one or the other, would you rather be rich or famous?

There is no magic wand

Many musicians think if they could just obtain the phone number to that record executive or major manager, all of their Disneyland dreams would come true. They could finally be the rock stars they deserve to be.

I have news for you. There is no magic wand. No magic phone number. And chances are all the conversations in the world won't make your music better. Focus on creating the best music you possibly can. Focus on putting on the best live performance. Make the best recordings. Market your band properly. Get those things in line first, and then worry about making the contacts. Chances are if you do those things well, the contacts will come to you.

Bands often think that if they could just get that booking agent on the phone, they'd finally be able to tour. Not true. If you're doing the numbers by selling out venues, trust me, you're going to have no problem getting that booking agent on the phone.

> *Cousin Rick says:* If you are an original artist, write a song this week. It doesn't need to be your masterpiece. Just write a song this week. If you're a cover band musician, learn a new song this week.

Would they sell their worldly possessions just to hear your music?

I was already 19 before I attended my first real concert. It was Stryper. Yes, *that* Stryper -- the '80s Christian hair-rock band that threw Bibles into the audience and dressed in yellow and black outfits. It was 1986.

My first rock show was not necessarily a concert. Prior to that, I had only seen bands play in bars. My first bar show experience was at a small music venue in Raleigh called The Switch, where I saw a popular cover band called Sidewinder. I was in the front row near the bass player, Robert Kearns. Robert went on to play in The Bottle Rockets, Lynyrd Skynyrd, and Sheryl Crow. The guitar player in that band was Audley Freed, who later became the guitarist for The Black Crowes and Sheryl Crow along with a long list of notable country stars. Not a bad first-rock-show experience for it being a cover band at a club in Raleigh, North Carolina. They definitely set the bar high.

Anyway, back to Stryper...

My best friend, David McCreary, knew the DJ for the Christian rock radio show at East Carolina University that aired every Sunday morning. David introduced me to this DJ, Mark Barber. At the time, Mark was probably the most famous person I had ever met in my life. He was on the radio and the host of his own weekly show. Mark was about as cool as a person could be. He was the only person I knew who had long hair. He was a good-looking guy so he always had pretty girls around him. He had charisma that just drew you into his world, and Mark's world was music.

The thing Mark was most excited about was this new band called Stryper. Stryper's record label had sent him copies of their new album to give away on the air, and he gave my friend David and me a copy. Up to this point in my life, aside from my cousin Rick many years earlier, I had never seen someone so cool get so excited about music. If someone this cool got excited about a band, it must be good.

Because of Mark, I began listening to Stryper and loved it. It was my kind of thing. Great music, awesome songs, a unique look, and they sang a positive message. I was raised in the church and didn't really relate to songs about the devil, drugs or mayhem. Sure, I liked Poison, Mötley Crüe, Bon Jovi, and all the others of that era. But their lyrics seemed foreign to this small-town, God-fearing teenager. I had never seen girls, girls, and girls at a strip club. I had never talked dirty to a girl in the basement or in my old man's Ford. I wasn't a cowboy nor did I ride a steel horse. No, I grew up in a small church community, and I didn't really do all the wild things that many teenagers did. So when I heard Stryper sing a message of "It's okay to be a good person and still rock," now *that* I could relate to.

Time passed and I continued to listen to Stryper. Finally, they toured the East coast. They were coming to Spartanburg, South Carolina, which was about a 5-hour drive from where I was living. This was going to be my first concert. There was only one problem. I was broke. I was a freshman in college and my bank account was empty. So I did what any young freshman would do who wanted to go to a rock concert but didn't have the money -- I asked my dad for it.

And like any good dad, he said, "I won't give you the money, but I'll tell you what. If you clean out the garage, there's a stereo in there you can have." So I cleaned the garage. I got the stereo, marched straight down to the local pawnshop, and sold it for $25. I got enough money to buy a ticket and some gas for the car.

We piled four people in the car and hit the road. We arrived hours early as it was a general admission concert and we wanted to be in the front row, and eventually we were. The doors opened and we rushed the stage. I was planted stage right, in front of bassist Timothy Gaines. That concert was everything I had hoped it would be and more. I knew I just *had* to be a part of all of this. I knew I wanted to somehow be in music. I wasn't sure if I wanted to play music or what, but I knew *this* life was for me.

Fast-forward to 2003, I managed the reunited Stryper on their first-ever tour since they had broken up in 1991. I played a lead role in orchestrating the reunion of the band that I once sold a stereo just to see in concert. Just writing that sentence seems surreal.

Yes, I sold a stereo to get money for tickets and gas, so that I could drive 5 hours, just to hear a band in concert. Oh, and by the way, we drove 5 hours back after the concert, too. We certainly didn't have enough money for a hotel.

Would people do that for your music? Would they sell their worldly possessions just for the opportunity to hear your music?

That's exactly what you are asking people to do when you want them to pay a cover charge to come hear your band at a bar. You are saying to them, "I realize you work hard all day. But I'm going to ask you to give me part of your hard earned money so that you can have the opportunity to listen to my music."

Is your music really that damn good? It had better be. It'd better be brilliant. Because if total strangers aren't willing to sell their stereo and drive 5 hours to hear you in concert, then you have more songs that you need to write and record.

Never forget that whether it's a $5 cover charge at a bar, a $10 CD purchase, or a $55 ticket at an amphitheater, you should be extremely grateful to each and every person who ever spends money on your music. Because they may very well have just cleaned their dad's garage and sold a stereo just to hear it.

Me, Michael Sweet and David McCreary.
We arrived so early to the show that we were able to meet Michael going in to sound check.
24 hours earlier I had just sold a stereo in order to be at this show.

> *Cousin Rick says:* This week choose one of your active fans and give him or her something for free, asking nothing in return, just to show appreciation. It could be a T-shirt, an unreleased recording, or even something unrelated to your band like tickets to a local sporting event.

"Why am I doing this?"

Don't forget to remind yourself on a regular basis why you are in the music business. I often tell people, "I didn't choose music. It chose me." If you are in this truly for the love of music, for the pursuit of fulfilling your every creative desire, then remind yourself of that on a daily basis.

One of my favorite movies is called *Bandwagon* (directed by John Schultz, if you're looking it up. And I highly recommend you do). In that movie is a tour manager named Linus Tate (played by Doug McMillan of The Connells) who ultimately takes a young band called Circus Monkey under his wing.

His first encounter with Circus Monkey is after one of their shows. Linus is shooting pool in the back room of the venue and the band asks him (as bands so often do when seeking approval of experienced industry veterans), "So what'd you think? Do you think we've got what it takes?"

Linus Tate responds with, "Depends. Depends on what you wanna do."

Confused, the band presses him to elaborate.

"Well, is music an end, or a means to an end?" Tate asks.

Still somewhat confused the band presses on.

Linus continues shooting pool as he says, "Am I here to shoot balls or to clear the table?"

This little lesson is something bands need to remind themselves of daily. What IS your purpose? Is the music the goal? Or is it a path to the goal?

If your goal is wealth and fame, I might suggest you take another path. Finance, maybe. Or technology. Acting or medical work. Anything but music. Because music is one of the most difficult and least likely ways to achieve fame and fortune.

The reason there are so many musicians is because the music *is* the goal. If you're in this for the music, then as long as you are creating and playing music, aren't you already successful?

Be in it for the music. Remember why you are in this on a daily basis. Don't ever forget it. Because if you do, it will become the most frustrating career path you could have ever chosen. And when roadblocks get in your way -- because they will -- they won't seem so daunting. Constantly remind yourself that you are already doing what you love. You are already successful. You are making music.

Chapter 2:
Don't Be an Idiot

The top three artists of all time

I've heard countless famous musicians say that the process of "making it" was, in many cases, more fun than the arrival of stardom. It's true. Make the journey an enjoyable one.

If you have gotten into music for any other reason than the love of music, the process will likely frustrate you beyond belief. Love your craft and love the process.

Once you've defined what your idea of success is, you need to start laying the groundwork step by step to make that happen. One of my most common suggestions is to examine the careers of artists you admire. If you were to play on the big stage, which big-name act would you share fans with?

Study the careers of the greats. Pick your top three artists of all time (artists whom you would like to have a career like- not necessarily artists you'd like to mimic musically, but whose career path you respect and admire). Now, learn everything you possibly can about those artists. Their life, their path, their journey. You'll find that most career-artists have worked very hard at their craft playing many thousands of hours before even getting to the starting line of the music business race.

Local bands come in all shapes and sizes. Your idea of success is likely different than that of others. But if you have defined it clearly, you can set out to do what you want by making short-term and long-term goals.

If you're a cover band wanting to play higher paying shows, go to the shows of those higher paying bands and learn everything you can.

I once met a guy who wanted to turn his struggling cover band into one that made good money. He drove three hours one night to sit in the back of the room and write down every song played by the top cover band in the region. He came back to his band mates with a list of brand new songs to learn.

If you're an original band, you're likely writing your own music. My suggestion to original bands is write, write, and write. Always be writing and demoing your songs.

Furthermore, I highly recommend co-writing. Surely there are songwriters in other local bands that you admire. Go to their shows. Meet them. Let them know you admire their songwriting. And ask if they'd be interested in writing a song with you. Most will. Not all of them will, but keep trying. Tell them you are writing for your next record and that you'd be thrilled if they could take a day to co-write with you.

The biggest thing to come out of co-writing isn't always the song. It's finding new ways to approach writing. It's getting your mind to think of new and creative ways to structure songs, create lyrics, and develop arrangements. Co-writing isn't just about walking away with *the* song, it's about learning new ways of writing, and developing relationships along the way.

All local bands that have defined their own success as millions of records sold or appearing on the radio charts, should co-write on a regular basis.

If you're an original band, don't quit your day job. It's likely going to be the catalyst to supporting your hobby, and that's exactly what it is right now -- a hobby. Don't fool yourself into believing millions of dollars are just around the corner because you've got some fans and great music.

I talk a lot about cover bands versus original bands. It's entirely possible to do both. I manage a local band right now that plays out under a pseudonym as a cover band to make money for their recordings and travel as an original band. I encourage this. It keeps your chops up. It keeps you playing music. Not to mention, by playing covers you are likely playing the music of some of the greatest artists of all time and thus picking up on song structures, chord changes, and lyrics that made them the greats that they are.

Just don't lose focus of your definition of success. If you want to be an original band playing your own music and making money with it, but you want to do a cover band on the side to make "rent money," don't let the cover band take over your world. Keep your eye on the prize. But whether it's a day job or a cover band on the side, you're going to need a way to make a living.

> *Cousin Rick says:* Who are the three greatest bands or artists of all time? This week, read something about each of those bands, paying particular attention to their early career paths.

When opportunity knocks, where will you be?

Too many musicians don't know when to seize the moment. When opportunity knocks, answer the damn door.

Allow me to tell you a story about the band Parmalee. This band is the perfect example of doing everything by the book, yet still having a rocky road to a career in music. They did everything by the book. I signed them to a management deal in 2000. It took 11 years before they finally got a record deal, and it all came down to knowing how to seize that moment.

During their 11-year path they did everything right. Parmalee was a rock band. They had an album produced by David Bendeth (Breaking Benjamin, Papa Roach, 12 Stones, Paramore, Vertical Horizon, etc.). They had songs co-written with and produced by Nikki Sixx of Motley Crue. They even had a stint where they were managed by the guys in Papa Roach. They had huge presence on the Internet, a loyal regional fan base, and they had showcased for every record label under the sun. All the elements were there. Great songs. Big fan base. They surrounded themselves with the right people. But for some reason, it never translated to the masses.

Matt Thomas of Parmalee and I

One day, a guy from South Carolina named Benton Blount recorded a country album and decided to cover one of Parmalee's songs, "Carolina." The buzz was stirring in Nashville that this Benton guy was going to get big on the radio with this song... a song written by Parmalee.

This was the moment.

"Carolina" had not yet been released to radio. And anyone who knows country radio knows that a song can come and go within a matter of weeks. The industry was buzzing about this song, but it had not yet been released to the public.

So, I called the guys in Parmalee and said, "You should go to Nashville and write while the buzz is hot on your song. God forbid, should the song flop, at least you will have gotten some other co-writing in before it does. If it does happen to hit, even better, you can continue writing for others."

After 11 years, Parmalee was ready. I give them all the credit in the world for this. Within a days notice, they had packed their bags and were off to Nashville to write. Thanks to a former Deep South employee and good friend, Greg Gallo, they connected with some great writers in Nashville. One thing led to another (all in a matter of a few days) and Parmalee ended up writing some songs with the production team behind country stars Jason Aldean and Thompson Square.

Within a relatively short amount of time, they signed a recording contract with Stoney Creek Records. However, after the co-writing sessions but before the record deal, they were met with even more hardship. The drummer, Scott Thomas, was the victim of a robbery shooting leaving him hanging on for his life (research that story. That story alone could be an entire book). Their tour RV was demolished by a fallen tree. Bills and debt accrued to levels that seemed to be insurmountable.

All of these were great reasons for them to say "Eh, we gave it a good shot," and give up. But they didn't. One of Scott's first shows after the shooting was their label showcase.

There is a lot more to that story, but the point is this: the opportunity was right for Parmalee. They had a short buzz window where their song, recorded by another artist, would either hit the charts or flop. That short window was their best opportunity to get in with some brilliant writers and producers... and so they did.

They didn't make excuses.

"I have to work."

"We're short on money right now."

"Let's wait until next month."

"We're going to Nashville just to write songs? We can do that here in North Carolina."

No, there was none of that. They *knew* this was a moment where they needed to act. It was uncertain. There were no guarantees. Actually, it was very likely that nothing at all would come out of this trip to Nashville. But they knew they had to try. They gave it their best shot and it worked. Parmalee, throughout their career, never passed up an opportunity to seize the moment. Prior to this, they had seized many moments, never knowing which one might pay off.

The label that signed Benton Blount, the artist who recorded the Parmalee song, went out of business before the song even went to radio. Had Parmalee waited another 2 weeks to go to Nashville, their shining moment as writers would have come and gone, and it's very unlikely they would have connected with the people they did.

Parmalee went on to have a #1 Billboard Country single with their song "Carolina," the song that had set them on this journey several years earlier. Parmalee now has a career in music. They persevered and seized every opportunity possible, and it paid off.

I was talking with an artist on the phone the other day who is actually friends with the members of Parmalee. She called me as a friend, just to get some advice - and vent. She was sharing with me her frustration that her career wasn't "taking off" quite fast enough. I said, as I will probably say to many artists in the future, "Do what Parmalee did. You should do exactly what they did when they felt like you. When they got frustrated, down in the dumps, and discouraged - You should do exactly what they did in those moments."

Knowing the guys in the band, she asked me if she had overlooked some major element of their life.

"What's that? What *did* they do?"

She asked that question very genuinely, as if they had some magic wand that she had overlooked.

"They just kept doing it," I said. "They just kept making music even when they probably didn't feel like it at times. They kept playing dive bars, often to small crowds. They continued to not complain, but to try to find the opportunity in every situation. But mostly, they just kept doing it."

And why did they keep doing it? Because when music is the goal, not a means to a goal, then that's what you do; you just keep making music because it's in your blood.

Seize the moment. Don't get caught up in the wrong stuff. If you're not careful, the things you think are important (but really aren't) will consume all of your time. And when opportunity knocks, you'll be out in the backyard smoking a joint and won't even hear the bang at the door.

> *Cousin Rick says:* Pick a dollar amount that you can put into a savings account each month. Maybe it's $5, $50, or $500 a month. Whatever the amount is, stick to it. When opportunity knocks, it will rarely be holding a bag of money at the door. Be prepared.

Communication

Learn to be a good communicator. If you're a band, designate the best communicator in the group to be the liaison between your band and other businesses, agents, managers, venues, etc.

A rapid-fire email sent from your mobile device reading "Whaddup? Got n e nights open at ur bar? We r ready 2 play" is not good communication. Read and re-read the emails you send. Be polite on the telephone. Don't expect anything. Say "Thank You." Use the common courtesy your grandmother tried to teach you.

One aspect of good communication, particularly when reaching out to an agent, record label, or manager, is to do your research. I'm amazed at how many emails I get from bands or musicians pitching something that has nothing to do with my business model. For example, my company does not book original bands. We are not a booking agency for original bands. So I'm shocked at the number of original acts that email me saying, "We're looking for an agent. Are you interested?" No, I'm not interested. It's not even what we do. Now I'm even less interested because you didn't take the time to research that on your own.

We live in an Internet world where a few clicks of the mouse can help you find out almost anything you want to know about the company you are getting ready to call or send a message. Don't expect those companies to take you seriously if you haven't taken the time to do your homework first.

For several years my company was fortunate enough to manage one of America's great rock bands, Little Feat. I have the utmost respect for the entire band, but I always got along really well with founding member Bill Payne. I've always known Bill to be a great communicator, and so I asked him to give advice to aspiring musicians, and he graciously allowed me to re-print something he wrote for Player Magazine:

> *"I have watched the odd dance between music and business for a long time. This is the dance of politics and music. All the rules and mentality of business and politics apply: leverage, the art of negotiation, toughness, persistence, understanding scope and parameters, presentation and style, flexibility, compromise, dealing with rejection, learning to actually embrace rejection as a means of growth, renewal, reinvestment, patience, the will to survive. Of course, many of these are, or should be, part of the artist mind set as well. I have been guilty of letting the "experts" make the calls, only to see my hopes dashed on the rocks. My life's work depends upon the business decisions being made in a way that supports my desire to create.*
>
> *We tend to adopt roles: I am a musician; he is my manager. There*

is a sense of staying out of others sacred territory; letting the "experts" handle it because they'll know what I want. Of course, there is the intersection of ideas and communication, but often times I have trusted my business associates to see, hear, and interpret a variety of issues as I do. I have done this without making it clear what it is I really want, or being patient enough to make sure they have heard my message and understand it. Big mistake.

My analogy is this: I wouldn't let a plumber into my house and say, "Whatever you want to fix, go ahead." What I say is, "There's a leak in the kitchen sink faucet, can you take a look at it and tell me what you think it will take to fix it...oh, and how much will it cost?" And yet, many artists complain loud and long (me being one of them) about all the ills done to us by people working on our behalf. The question is, how much help were we to our cause, or did we leave it to others to read into our desires? I have come up with the conclusion that I need to be a better partner with the people I work with."

-Bill Payne (Little Feat)

> *Cousin Rick says:* Before sending your next business e-mail, ask a friend who is a talented writer to review your email and offer feedback, edits, and input. Even the best of communicators can use improvement. The more important the subject matter, the more important it is to get input from others before sending.

Network, network, network

Get out and meet people. Meet musicians. Meet industry people. Meet radio people. You have to be proactive. They aren't going to seek you out.

Networking provides you the opportunity to pick up on little pieces of information that can help with the big picture. There is no magic wand. There is no rabbit in the hat that will make you successful, whatever your definition of success may be. Instead, there are little nuggets of gold placed in every corner of this industry that you need to find. You find those by talking to people.

Go to shows and meet bands you believe are heading down the right path, and don't be afraid to ask a few questions. Maybe you want to know who to talk to at a venue about getting a show. Or maybe you want to know who prints their T-shirts.

Go to radio functions. Almost every Saturday around America, your local radio station is set up somewhere to do a remote broadcast. It may be at a tech store, or it may be at a grocery store. Almost always the on-air talent from these radio stations are present at these events. Go meet them. Talk to them.

Let's not forget music conferences. Today, the granddaddy of them all is SXSW (South by Southwest), but conferences like that are scattered all over the world. Sign up. Go to them. Meet as many people as possible and learn as much as you can.

You don't need to travel the world to get this information. A lot of it is right at your fingertips on the Internet. However, the Internet will never replace human interaction with others in the same business as you. Get out and meet others in the industry on a regular basis.

While you're out there meeting people, be nice to *everyone*, always. The music business is a very small world. Do not think to that you will never cross paths with these people again. You will. So be nice to them on the way up, and they'll be nice to you on your way down -- that is when you'll need them the most.

This was my early attempt at networking with Geoff Tate of Queensryche. I gave him my demo tape and he was nice about it. Hopefully one day I'll have the opportunity to be nice back to him. I've not met him since this day backstage at one of his shows in the early '90s.

> *Cousin Rick says:* In the next 30 days, go to an event for the sole purpose of networking. Then follow-up with the people you met at that event.

Q: *Afton from Mobile, AL asks: I am a singer/songwriter and interested in forming a band around my songs. Any suggestions on how to go about doing this?*

A: Some say that a band is like a marriage between a group of people. In the beginning, when you're a young solo artist, it's more like dating, or perhaps even just going to the school dance.

Don't seek out a band that you plan to marry and spend the rest of your life with. Date around first.

Start by asking friends. Just talk to people you like and respect. Good people tend to surround themselves with good people. Ask people you like if they know any musicians looking for a band.

Depending on what stage you are at in your career, you can go about this in different ways. If you're just starting out without much of a following, plan on your band also performing with other bands. It's rare to get a band to commit strictly to you, especially when you don't have a lot to offer. But that's okay. As you grow, hopefully they will grow with you.

If you're an established solo artist, finding a band might come a little easier.

Don't be afraid to post "wanted" ads on the Internet. My primary advice here is to be as specific as possible in your ad. Don't take out an ad that says "Singer / Songwriter looking for a drummer." You're going to get all sorts of unwanted responses with an ad like that.

Here are some guidelines for a good ad:

Specifically describe your music using as much detail as possible, or better yet offer a link for people to listen.

How often do you play out? And do you want to play more than you do currently?

What are your short and long term goals?

Do you want musicians with a certain playing style, fashion style, or age-range? If so, specifically describe each.

Do you want musicians that live in your area? If so, talk about the area where you live, play out, and rehearse.

Do you make money? How much do you plan to pay these musicians, if anything? Discuss that topic in your ad.

Do you currently tour? Some musicians can't travel. And just because you one day hope to tour, don't discount someone because they can't travel. Almost everyone would happily quit their day job for the right tour. Worry about making great music first. Cover these things in your ad, and it will eliminate a lot of unwanted responses.

Make a list

If you are a musician hoping to have a career in music, you're going to need to regularly check your progress along your path to success. Lists are a great way to do that.

I have two types of to-do lists in my life. One is a daily list and the other is an annual list.

Every morning I take a minute or two to jot down the things I need to accomplish <u>today</u>. Sometimes throughout the evening I will even email myself adding items to my to-do list. A daily to-do list is a great way to keep me moving in a forward direction, because if you're doing this right -- if you're truly headed for a career in music -- you are going to have a gazillion things coming at you at once. Without a list to keep you focused, it's easy to fall off course.

My daily lists usually consist of things like:

- ✓ Call John, Allison, Fred, Doug, and Jeff.
- ✓ Finish reviewing the contract and send notes to the attorney.
- ✓ Schedule a meeting with Jim about the website.
- ✓ Pick up an electric screwdriver at the hardware store (Okay, so not *all* of my life is about music).
- ✓ Call the agent about an update on the tour.

You get the idea. My daily lists are things I want to get done *today*. I try to keep it short and realistic, knowing new topics will hit my desk throughout the day. If you make a list every day, you won't get overwhelmed. If you don't complete a task, don't be discouraged. Just carry it forward to tomorrow's list.

I make my annual to-do list at the beginning of every year. Ten things I want to accomplish that year. Some things are personal, and some are professional. I try not to exceed 10 because it can get too overwhelming if I have too many. Pick a number that is right for you. Don't mistake this for a New Year's Resolution. New Year's Resolutions are typically open-ended and unrealistic. Be specific with your lists. Instead of saying "Write more songs," say "Write 20 songs." Instead of saying "Lose weight," say "Lose 8 pounds." Be specific.

Throughout the year, as you accomplish something on that list, cross it off. Celebrate your victory. Recognize it by sharing your accomplishment with a friend. If you only have 10 goals on your annual list, each one should be a great victory. Don't let it drift quietly into the night. Celebrate it by telling a friend about the passing of this mile marker.

I've put together a checklist of sorts for you. Below are some things you need to make sure you complete on your path to having a career as a musician.

YOUR CHECKLIST TO SUCCESS

- ✓ Learn how to play your instrument well.
- ✓ Now learn how to play it even better.
- ✓ Nope. We are not there yet. Get a little bit better.
- ✓ Define your idea of success in extreme detail. Write it down, and hang it in a visible place where you will see it daily.
- ✓ Record three songs every 3 to 4 months (don't spend a lot of money).
- ✓ Make a video for one of those songs each time you record (don't spend a lot of money).
- ✓ Create an impressive and professional Internet presence for you and your music (don't spend a lot of money).
- ✓ Take new photos of you or your band every 3 to 6 months (don't spend a lot of money).
- ✓ Anyone can be on the Internet. Make your presence known. Network daily on the Internet.
- ✓ Perform live regularly. You won't succeed by playing gigs.

You'll succeed by being brilliant at your art. To be brilliant, you need to log thousands of hours practicing your art in front of an audience. In the beginning, play anywhere you can. And as you grow, still continue to play, but by expanding into new markets.

✓ Once a day, attempt to introduce your music to one new industry person. This may include a venue owner, a booking agent, a producer, another musician, or anyone who has any ties at all to the music business.

✓ Make at least five phone calls per day pertaining to your business and your path to success.

✓ At least once a month, go hear another band or musician in a live performance. One who you believe is headed in the right direction on their career path. It's amazing what you can learn just by watching others on a regular basis.

✓ Play a show for charity. Pick a charity and offer your talents. Perform at no charge. Do this once a year.

✓ If you aspire to be a songwriter, co-write with anyone and everyone that is willing to co-write with you. You may just end up with a great song. And you'll most likely learn something new about how to approach writing. Regardless, you will strengthen yourself as a writer and as a person by experiencing new ideas and situations.

✓ Have fun, daily. If it's no longer fun for you on a regular basis, quit. Music is supposed to be fun and part of your soul. Do things to keep it fun. Be aware of whether or not you are enjoying the process. You'd be amazed how many musicians will let years go by before they wake up to realize they no longer enjoy their profession. In many cases, they probably would have enjoyed it more just by making themselves consciously aware of their feelings. Check yourself and the level of fun you are having on a regular basis. Keep it fun, whatever your idea of fun is.

✓ Learn a secondary instrument. No need to master it, just learn to explore something other than your primary instrument. I'm a bass player. Learning a little about how to play the drums helped me tremendously with my bass playing. I also learned a little guitar and piano. Each time I learned something on an instrument other than bass, I felt as if a brand new world had opened up to me. Again, no need to master secondary instruments, just enjoy the process of learning how to play them.

Use this as a guideline to make your own checklists. Cater it to your definition of success.

> *Cousin Rick says:* Make a list of only three things that you want to have done tomorrow. Stay focused on that list throughout the day. If successful, expand that list to four things the next day, and so on until your lists are realistic and manageable.

Look the part

There are those in the industry who will tell you, "It's all about the music."

I'm not one of them.

No doubt, the music is *the* most important part. Without great music you may have your 15 minutes of fame, but you don't have fans -- not long-term ones at least. Without a solid fan base, a career in music is not possible.

Maintain your music career as you would your car. The music is the engine. You *must* have a great engine. Without it, you really don't have much to sustain. But a great engine alone won't make a great car. You need a steering wheel, brakes, tires, a rust-free frame to support it, and it never hurts to have a nice paint job. Not to mention you need to maintain your car. Wash it regularly. Oil changes, tune-ups, and regular maintenance are all necessary to keep your car in tip-top shape.

You can have the cleanest car with the best set of tires and paint job, but if you have a shoddy engine, it's just not going to sustain you for very long. It might get the girls looking at you for a little while, but that will soon pass without a good engine to get you where you're going.

A music career must have great music. Without great, inspiring music, all you've got is the shell of a car and nowhere to go. But while you're obtaining virtuosity, you've got to pay attention to the other parts of the car as well. How you dress matters.

For example, I'd be skeptical if I went to see my mechanic and he was wearing a three-piece suit. I'd question my banker if I went to his office and he was wearing flip-flops and a tank top. I'm not sure I'd want my tennis instructor wearing a leather vest and motorcycle boots. My doctor should look like a doctor. My plumber should look like a plumber.

And, for the love of God, we want our rock stars to look like rock stars.

Sounds easy enough, right? Easier said than done.

There are so many different fashion styles within the entertainment industry, finding the style that works for you may not come as easy as you'd like. But just like writing great music, work on it. It'll come.

When dealing with a band, getting a group of musicians to agree on a style for the band can be difficult.

There are no rules on what to wear. The best advice I give bands is to talk about it. Spend time working on your style, your image. Spend twenty minutes not playing your instruments and talk about your image. Make it a priority. The biggest mistake bands make is ignoring the topic altogether.

Again, you can have a great looking car, but without an engine it's meaningless. Don't lose focus on the engine: the songs. You can't ignore the appearance of your car either.

I like to play a game with bands called "Which One Is Not Like the Others?"

When I see a band struggling with their image (even though they may not know it themselves) I will take their promo picture and put in on a table alongside four other national bands that would fit into their style of music.

Five pictures are lying on the table. Four of them national recording artists and one of them is the local artist who wants to figure out how to hit the big time.

I say to the local artist, "If I were to ask a six-year-old to play a game of 'Which One Is Not Like the Others?' how hard do you think it would be for them to tell which of these five pictures doesn't belong?"

It's usually easy to tell the difference. I say to bands, "When a six-year-old would have a hard time figuring out which picture doesn't belong, *then* you're on the right track to portraying a good image for your music."

Most bands just don't think about it. They don't talk about it, and that's a problem. You *must* discuss your image.

A local cover band once asked me to come hear them and give my feedback, so I went to a sports bar where they were performing. They were AMAZING! They were an incredible band playing all the right cover songs. The problem was that they wanted to be playing weddings and corporate gigs instead of sports bars.

The band was wearing jeans and T-shirts during their performance, which was appropriate for a sports bar, but they didn't want to be playing in sports bars.

After the show, the band gathered around in hopes I'd have the solutions to all their problems. I was going to wave my magic wand and somehow transform them from playing sports bars to the high-dollar world of corporate gigs and weddings.

They wanted my feedback. So, I said, "You've got the music. That's no problem. You sound as good as any cover band in the area. You've obviously been working hard and it shows. My main suggestion, though, is you need to clean up your image if you want to play corporate shows and weddings."

The singer leaned back, crossed his arms and retorted, "You get me a big money gig and I'll wear anything you want me to wear."

That is the problem most local bands face, be it original or cover bands. They have it backwards. They think somehow they get the "big gig" first, and *then* put on the nice suits.

Look the part you want to play, then you get the gig. Not the other way around. If you're an original act looking for that big record deal, don't think that you can wait until that happens to start concentrating on your image. If you're a cover band hoping for the higher paying corporate performances, don't wait until you get the gig to start wearing the nice suit. It won't happen. You must look the part first.

Dress for the gig you want, not the gig you have.

If you're a cover band playing sports bars and want to be playing corporate shows, look the part of a corporate band while playing the sports bars. Force the audience in the sports bar to say to themselves, "This band doesn't look like they belong here. They look like they should be playing some big festival or fancy corporate performance." *That* is when you'll start to get those gigs.

Try this fun test to gauge the effectiveness of your image: When arriving to play a show at some local dive bar, if the door guy asks to see your I.D., you're probably not dressing the part. Dress in a way that the door guy will say, "You must be with the band."

The most important thing is to think about and discuss your image on a regular basis. Don't leave it to chance. Make it a part of your career-building path. And remember what I said: dress for the gig you want, not the gig you have.

Once you've gone through the process of creating a great image, don't ruin it by not having a good promo picture. Every city has a surplus of talented photographers willing to expand their portfolio. Don't take a quick snapshot on a railroad track or in front of the brick wall behind your practice space. Spend time on a photo shoot, and make it great.

Embarrassing picture #2
In 1988, "looking the part" meant putting on make-up.

Q: *Johnny from Charlotte, NC asks: Which is more important: music, lyrics, or image?*

A: The answer to this really does depend on your style of music, but all three elements are necessary for success. Don't discount one over the other. Lyrics and image tend to often take a back seat.

I was managing a band on Wind-Up Records and I watched the President of that label go through every single line of every single song reading the lyrics for new releases. He was great at knowing what the public could relate to, and that's exactly how he read lyrics. Can the public relate to this? If so, he kept it. If not, he encouraged change. This, of course, was for a pop-rock band. Lyrics are very important if you're going for a pop audience, be it rock, country, or R&B. If you want your songs to be loved by the masses, the lyrics are going to need to appeal to the masses.

There are plenty of catchy songs that have never made it simply because the intended audience could not relate to the lyrical content.

For many artists, image often takes the back seat. To some artists it's an after-thought. Without great music and lyrics, you can have the greatest image in the world and it won't matter. You need great music and lyrics first, but pay equally as much attention to your image. Your audience wants to relate to you.

There are exceptions for every rule in the imaging department, but generally speaking you should look the part that fans of your music would expect. Sure, be as creative with your image as you are with your music, but don't alienate the fans.

Very few fans of jazz music envision their favorite jazz songwriters to be wearing nose rings, tattoos all over themselves, and a "Kill 'Em All" T-shirt. If you're going to play jazz music, look the part of a jazz musician.

Not one of these elements -- music, lyrics, or image -- is more important than the other. They're all important and need to work together in creating your brand.

Cousin Rick says: If you are in a band, schedule a band meeting to take place this week and do nothing but talk about your image. If you are a solo artist, gather some trusted friends and discuss your image with them. Ask for opinions and help.

8 hours of sleep

How in the world could the time I wake up possibly matter to the success of my musical career? The most successful musicians I know wake up at a reasonable hour. In fact, most successful people I know in any profession wake up early.

There's a definitive correlation between success and not sleeping your day away. The obvious reason would be because you can get more done when you're not sleeping 12 hours a day. That stands to reason, but that's not *the* reason.

Maybe you're a working musician and perform until 2 am every night. Or maybe you're an out of work musician and just stay up late rehearsing or writing songs. Staying up late is okay, but no matter what time you go to bed, don't let your sleep become an open-ended time period. Set an alarm for roughly 8 hours after you go to bed and get up when that alarm goes off.

Then, once up, spend the first 15 minutes of your day doing something that has nothing to do with music. This is *your* time. Do not read your emails. Do not answer your phone. Do not pick up your guitar. Do something you love, besides music. Go for a jog. Water your garden. Read some pages in a book. Or just have a cup of coffee and do nothing, for 15 minutes.

Your typical day should be filled with a lot of work, phone calls, and emails. When you take 15 minutes of *your* time to start the day -- time that nobody can take away from you -- it allows you to be more focused throughout the day. You will feel less stressed and rushed because you know you've taken that moment of free time all to yourself, doing anything you want with it. You won't feel nearly as agitated or rushed to complete the day's tasks if you know you've had some "you" time.

Most people you will work with in the music business wake up early. Get on their radar early in the day. If you have an agent, call or email him. If you're booking yourself, make calls and send emails early in the day. No matter where you are in your career, there are people you need to be talking to who work regular business hours. The earlier you can get to them, the better.

I have a very successful booking agent friend of 20 years who has set a strict rule for himself throughout his career. His rule is: make 20 outgoing phone calls before noon, and the rest of the day will dictate itself.

It's true. The first part of your day dictates how the rest of it will play out. Agents, clubs, labels, managers... they all have very busy days.

If you're on their morning list, you're much more likely to get their attention.

Michael Sweet (of Stryper and formerly of BOSTON) is one of my clients. Like clockwork, he calls me every morning before 11 am. We run through topics and goals and it really does set the tone for the day. I'm able to prioritize our to-do list and again, almost like clockwork, we touch base at the end of the day to re-cap our topics. And more often than not, we even have several phone conversations throughout the afternoon. All day long his business is on my to-do list. And yes, sometimes it gets a little overwhelming, but he's a guy who cares about his career and isn't afraid to pick up the phone and motivate those on his team.

I suppose it has all paid off, because Michael Sweet has sold over 8 million records.

Michael Sweet (of Stryper and formerly of BOSTON) and I

On the other hand, I also represent another artist who doesn't wake up until about 4 or 5 pm every day. I won't represent him much longer if he doesn't start waking up early. It's almost impossible to get anything done because by the time we finally talk, the business day has almost ended.

Most people with whom you work will only work as hard as you do. It's your career after all. Wake up early and show people you care about your career. Work hard, wake up early, and those around you will work hard as well.

> *Cousin Rick says:* Who are the three most successful people in any profession or business that you personally know? Ask them each what time they usually wake up in the morning and about how many hours of sleep they normally get per night.

How to spot an idiot

Don't be an idiot. Sounds pretty easy. Don't be stupid. As simple as this piece of advice might sound, you'd be surprised how many musicians just don't understand this very basic concept.

I compare this inability to judge whether or not *you* are the idiot to those signs you see hanging at fast food joints that say "Now hiring: Friendly people." When has anyone ever looked at those signs and said to themselves, "Damn, I'd really like a job at Burger World. If only I were friendly. Crap. Oh well"?

Everyone thinks they are friendly. And nobody thinks they're an idiot.

Every family has a weird uncle. If you think your family does not, then it's likely *you* are the weird uncle.

It's hard to tell if you are friendly, weird, or an idiot. But when it comes to succeeding in the music business, you need to be honest with yourself. Do you sometimes behave like an idiot?

Allow me to provide some specific examples on how not to be an idiot when you're in the beginning stages of your career. Don't send emails as if you were casually texting a good friend. Write in complete, coherent sentences.

On that same note, do not TYPE IN ALL CAPITAL LETTERS. You would think this is common sense by now, but apparently it's not. Just don't do it. If I need to explain why, you need to be reading another book -- perhaps one on proper communication in the Internet age.

When playing a venue for the first time, do not complain about *anything*. Period. Don't complain about the sound. Don't complain about the money. Don't complain about how many free beers you may or may not get. Be nice, appreciative, and engaging with the staff. If you don't like something about the venue, and it is something you just can't get past, then don't play there again. Chances are if you don't want to play a venue again, the feelings are likely mutual. But if they aren't, and the venue *does* ask you to play again, be honest but polite as to why you feel it's not the right fit for you.

> "Always make friends with the soundman."
> -Matt Thomas, *Parmalee*

Be persistent but not obnoxious. If you send your music to industry people, check back with them. Even checking back 3 or 4 times is okay. But after that, learn to take a hint. Most music industry people do their deals by way of phone and Internet, which means they pay attention to their calls and emails. Sure, we all miss an email or a phone message from time to time, which is why it's okay to check in a few times, but after that... take a hint. They're just not interested, and honestly probably don't have the time to tell you *why* they aren't interested. They're just not. Take a hint and move on.

On that note, don't expect full explanations as to why someone may not be interested. Let me put it in simple terms. I get anywhere from 10 to 15 submissions of new music or new bands every day. I would imagine many industry professionals receive more. Let's suppose it takes about 15 minutes to explain to a musician why I may not be interested, not to mention the time it takes to actually listen to the music. At that rate, it would take almost 4 hours of each day just to explain to each artist why I may not be interested. Just remember, if you send your music to an industry professional, don't expect an explanation as to why they may not be interested. Often times, it has nothing to do with you. Some people just may not feel like your music is the right fit for the company. Don't take it personally, or expect feedback, just move on.

Don't pass out flyers in a venue for your show at a competing venue.

Don't over-sell yourself. Sell yourself, yes. Just don't overdo it.

Don't put a lot of "fluff" in your electronic press kit or on your website. Industry people, and honestly even music fans, can see right through your fluff.

For example, if you played the side stage at the local amphitheater for the Dave Matthews Band show, *don't* say "Toured with Dave Matthews Band" on your website.

Be nice to people, treat them and their time with respect, believe in your art, and it's likely you will avoid falling into the "idiot" category.

Law & Order re-runs, basketball and gardening

You will drive yourself crazy if the *only* thing in your life is music. Sure, it should be a priority, but without a well-rounded lifestyle of non-music-related activities, you are going to become incredibly frustrated with not only the business of music, but also with life.

Bruce Hornsby plays basketball (and is actually *really* good. I remember hearing stories of him beating Allen Iverson once in one-on-one, and to the best of my knowledge, it's a true story). Allison Moorer makes clothing, writes short stories, and likes to cook. Vienna Teng also enjoys cooking and throwing the occasional dinner party. Michael Sweet likes working outside in his yard.

I "work" 7 days a week in the music industry. But I also like working in my yard, taking my Siberian Husky on walks in the woods, graphic design, and I like watching Law & Order re-runs with my girlfriend.

I *have* to do these things to keep a balance in my life. And so do you.

Don't think about music all the time. Think about it daily, but know when to put it down. Even if it's only for a short while each day, do something you love that has nothing to do with music.

My friend Philip Isley with Jewel. I like going to NC State Football games and Philip has season tickets. I'd like to think he takes me to the games because we're friends, but it's probably only because I introduced him to Jewel. (I'm kidding, Philip. Go Pack!)

Cousin Rick asks: What is your favorite thing to do that has nothing to do with music?

10 Things I learned from Bruce Hornsby (in no particular order)

1. There are ways to acknowledge your accomplishments in a humble manner. Often before a big concert or event, the local radio DJ or event spokesperson will announce the artist in advance, mentioning a few notable accolades of that artist. A typical introduction might be something like, "Please welcome to The Topeka Performing Arts Center, winner of the 2010 Best Artist in The World award, Hank Plank and The Two by Fours."

Early on in my relationship with Bruce, an event producer came to me saying, "Can you write down a brief introduction for Bruce that we can read off?" Being new with Bruce I wanted to run it by him first, and he told me exactly what he wanted the introduction to say. So I went back to the producer, gave him a handwritten piece of paper stating how Bruce would like to be introduced. He read it and looked up at me and said, "Are you serious? We can't say this! Won't he be upset?"

I said, "No, he'll love it. He wants to be introduced that way."

"Okay, if that's what he wants," the producer said skeptically.

Still, he asked me several more times before Bruce went on, "Are you sure about this? Really?"

"Yes, I'm sure. It'll be just fine. Just read the paper as it is."

So the lights dimmed and the event spokesperson came over the loud speaker and said, "Ladies and Gentlemen. Please welcome to the stage 10 time Grammy Nominee, 7 time loser, Bruce Hornsby."

2. Don't feel obligated to do things you don't want to do. Bruce made no apologies for turning down special functions, and Bruce gets asked to attend a *lot* of special functions. He would just say to me without apology, "No, thanks. That's just not my bag." People will respect you when you speak your mind.

3. The music matters. In modern times you will have people tell you that it's all about publicity, or marketing, or style. And to some extent those things are important, but without great music, nothing else matters. Practice your instrument to the point where you become an expert, and then practice it more.

4. Sports and music can be a lot alike. When Bruce is on stage, he challenges his band. He guides them like a point guard on a basketball team, taking them to places they have never been before. He transitions into brand new songs, or tries songs in different keys, and it keeps the band on their toes. He does this because he treats the stage like a basketball court, strengthening his team so they will always be ready for anything. And it shows. Competitive sports are a healthy part of life. Don't be afraid to put a little friendly competition in your music. Challenge those around you to play the best they've ever played by passing the ball to them when they least expect it.

5. Praise people that deserve praise. Bruce had no problem telling me when he felt like I didn't handle a situation properly. But he also had no problem publicly letting the team around him know when he liked the work I was doing.

6. Pick up the phone. It only happened to me once, and it was a lesson that stuck with me the rest of my life. Several key radio people needed tickets to his show. I was happy to oblige. So I emailed Bruce's tour manager giving him a list of the radio people who needed tickets and asked him to leave tickets at will call. The night of the show the tickets weren't at the will call. Bruce said to me, "Did you tell the tour manager?" And I said, "I emailed him." And Bruce said, "Pick up the phone and call him. Don't rely on email."

Although technology will continue to improve, nothing will ever beat a good old-fashioned conversation.

7. Take time for your family. Bruce always puts his family first.

8. Explore music with unlikely counterparts. Bruce started out as an '80s hit-maker, and then he played with The Grateful Dead. He did a lot of work with bluegrass legend Ricky Skaggs as well as jazz great Branford Marsalis. Step outside of your comfort zone to expand your abilities as a musician and songwriter.

9. Laugh at the music business, frequently. In one of Bruce's early interviews during our tenure together, he was asked if the business of music was frustrating. He explained that you just have to laugh a lot, and that if you take the music business too seriously it will drive you crazy. And it will. Don't take it too seriously. Learn to laugh at the industry when it deserves to be laughed at.

10. Words. I learned a lot of new words from Bruce. He made me sort of a hobbyist for learning new words. I learned a lot of new words from Allison Moorer as well. Both are avid readers and have an extremely deep knowledge of the English language. Bruce was the most erudite client of mine. I'm still not a word maven, but I strive to be, thanks to Bruce and Allison.

er·u·dite
adjective
Characterized by great knowledge; learned or scholarly: *an erudite professor; an erudite commentary.*

ma·ven
noun
An expert or connoisseur.

Chapter 3:
Record Labels. Who Cares?

Who's your boss?

If you worked at a bank or an insurance company, you would treat your boss with respect. You would listen to his or her opinion. You would value his or her input.

In the music business, the fans are your boss. Don't ever forget this. You wouldn't show up drunk to work at a bank for fear of your boss firing you. The same goes for a concert. Your fans are your boss. They have paid to come hear you. Respect your boss by giving them the best you have to give.

Everyone loves to be a rock star, but when you are performing for your boss -- your fans -- you need to be sober, alert, and appreciative.

Your fans spend their hard earned money to come to your concerts, buy your music and merchandise, and support your craft.

On those same lines, you need to regularly communicate with your boss(es). To do this, you need their information. A fan's email address is your most valuable marketing asset. Always put an email sign-up sheet out at every show. Maybe offer a free sticker or even some of your music if they'll give you their email address.

Don't abuse this information. Stay in touch with them regularly, but don't over-use your email list. Don't use your email list solely to tell your fans about shows. Engage them. Ask for feedback. Get their opinions. Your fans can help you correct mistakes before it's too late. Maybe you can get them involved listening to some new songs you've written. Or maybe they can help you pick a promo picture. Fans like to be involved, and they care.

Put your fans first. They are your boss; treat them with the utmost respect. Without them, you don't have a job.

Key West, FL
L to R: Dave Rose (Deep South), Shaun Murphy (Little Feat),
Bill Payne (Little Feat), Andy Martin (Deep South)

Little Feat is the best at giving back to their fans.
It's part of the reason why they've sustained a 30+ year career.

Cousin Rick says: Email one fan today that deserves a "thank you."

It's YOUR business. Be involved.

"I just wanna play music for a living and let other people worry about the business stuff," a local musician said to me recently.

Unfortunately, that will never be the case for this guy if he really wants to be successful. Musicians have to be business-savvy entrepreneurs, marketing experts, and great communicators. They also must be eager to be involved in every aspect of their career.

Think of yourself as the CEO of your own company. Although you may hate keeping up with your social media pages, sending emails to your fan base, or creating flyers to hang around town, you *have* to do these things.

You wouldn't start your own burger joint and say, "I only want to cook burgers. I don't want to mess with the money, the employees, the light bill, the salesman, the repairs, the landlord, etc." No, if your dream of all dreams is to own a burger joint, you will want and need to be involved in every aspect in order for it to be successful.

Musicians need to do the same. If you have decided that you want to be a band that plays music professionally, you must be involved in every aspect of your business, even the stuff you might not like.

Sure, as you get more popular you will have agents, lawyers, managers, and business managers to handle the vast majority of this work. But even then you will still need to be very involved in the decision-making process. The most successful artists I know are the ones who are involved on a daily basis in all aspects of their "company" (band). After all, it's *their* career that's on the line.

Allison Moorer would regularly attend business meetings alongside me. If I met with the record label, it was usually with her by my side. If I met with her attorney, it was usually with her by my side. That felt very natural to me -- having the artist actively involved in her business -- as it should. Sure, I handled a lot of daily business without her involvement, but if there were big decisions to be made that would affect her career or *her* business, she was there to play an active role in the process. I like that about her.

Don't fool yourself into thinking that there will come a day when all you think about is the music. It's career suicide to think about nothing but the music and not be involved in the other aspects of your career that aid in getting your music heard.

Allison Moorer and I

Avril

I like Avril Lavigne. There, I said it. I'm not necessarily speaking in terms of liking her as a person, although I do very much. More so, I like her dedication to her career. I was fortunate to get to know Avril when she was just starting out and I realized even then that she had the dedication, determination, and love for music that is needed for a career of her magnitude.

I first met Avril in 1999, just prior to her signing to Arista Records. Thanks to her then-manager (and friend of mine), Cliff Fabri, a huge buzz was building in the New York industry. Ken Krongard, also a friend and A&R at Arista, played a major role in getting LA Reid to ultimately sign her. But prior to the big recording contracts, she was just Avril.

It was a harsh winter day in Philadelphia when I first met up with Avril and Cliff at a music conference. We were all relatively new to the business and just trying to find our place in the world of music. As we bounced around from venue to venue, it was freezing cold with bone-chilling winds making matters worse. Being a southern boy, I didn't pack any sort of winter accessories like gloves or hats or scarfs. ASCAP, the performing rights organization, had a booth at the conference where they were giving away free embroidered knit caps, or beanies, as some may call them.

Throughout the day, I kept saying to Avril, "I need to go by the ASCAP booth and get one of those free toboggans." I said this multiple times throughout the day until finally, the Canadian-born Avril spoke up and said, "Why is ASCAP giving away sleds? It's not even snowing. Why do you want a sled?"

In the south a toboggan is a knit cap. In Canada it's a sled. We debated back and forth over the proper term for these knit caps. I insisted they were called toboggans. She insisted they were tuques. I had never even heard that word, tuque. Surely this young kid had no idea what she was talking about, I thought.

So we decided to settle the debate once and for all. We went into a drug store, where I was determined to not only purchase a toboggan, but also let an impartial third party (the drug store clerk) settle this disagreement. I found the section for toboggans (all the while, Avril insisting they were tuques) and picked out a nice blue one that would keep my ears cozy through the bitter Philadelphia weather. I walked to the counter, held up the cap and asked the older store clerk, "What do you call these?"

"I'm sorry? What do you mean?" the clerk said with a confused look on her face.

Still holding up the blue toboggan, I said, "*This*. What do you call *this* I'm holding in my hand?"

Looking around thinking she must be on a hidden-camera show of sorts, she hesitantly spoke up and said, "Uh... They're called knit caps."

Dangit. That didn't settle anything. Avril spoke up insisting it was a tuque. I rebutted insisting it was a toboggan. And the store clerk insisted we were both wrong saying, "No, I'm pretty sure it's neither. These are knit caps."

And so began the ongoing debate between Avril and I over tuque vs. toboggan.

We met up in New York months later, where Avril was beginning to seriously court Arista, with co-writing sessions being lined up for her throughout the city with some of the most acclaimed producers and songwriters. She took up residency in the city with her brother and manager, with no guarantee of a future in music, and gave her whole life to her dream. She was writing as often as she could, both with other writers and by herself. There were several nights when her friends were all out on the town, but she just stayed in to continue writing. She was, and is, dedicated completely to music. For Avril, music is the end goal, not a means to the end goal.

One particular evening, she managed to venture out to a mid-town steak restaurant which had a bar area near the front lobby. It was dark and loud. Loud music and loud conversation and a bit distracting in general. Her manager and several label representatives had brought her out to meet other industry executives. When a label or manager is considering working with an artist, they'll often introduce them in social settings with hopes of getting interest from industry peers.

This was just one of those nights, probably one of many that Avril had to endure. I say "endure" because Avril and I seemed to both dislike this setting. It was noisy, contrived, and not very interesting to either us. Despite me technically being one of the suits, I didn't and still don't really think like a suit. I like to think that my mind is more closely related to that of the artist. Yes, I can marry music and commerce, but if given the two, I understand the mind of an artist better than the mind of a stockbroker.

I can only assume Avril sensed this, because we quickly found ourselves in a world of our own -- talking about the industry, about her career, about her songs, and mostly how both of us would like to be somewhere other than this mahogany and dark leather steak house bar. Somehow, the conversation turned to her name. She asked if I felt she should go by just Avril, or should she use her full name and go by Avril Lavigne. We even considered the idea of a band name, and not using her name at all. We tossed back and forth the pros and cons of each, almost as if we were working through the solution together -- which we kind of were.

This is the way Avril operated. She was constantly considering the right move -- be it for a song, a producer, an outfit, or even her name. Even at her young age, she realized there are multiple parts to a career that need to be moving and working together in order to prove successful.

We both had concerns that the public wouldn't be able to properly pronounce Lavigne, or worse -- radio DJs wouldn't try and possibly avoid it all together. Had I had the wisdom then that I do now, I would have told her, "It really doesn't matter. Make great music and I promise they will learn how to pronounce your name." But I didn't have that wisdom then. I continued to weigh through the pros and cons with her.

Finally, seeing we weren't going to make much headway on leather couches while suits sipped Scotch, I decided to put some resolution to the conversation by saying "I've got it. I've got the answer to the name problem."

Her eyebrows raised and her eyes brightened with a bit of curiosity. She looked at me probably thinking, "Cool. Finally. I can cross this item off my to-do list. He sounds like he really does have the solution here."

"I've got it. I've got your name. This is what you're going to go by for the rest of your career and it's guaranteed to be a huge hit. People will love it," I teased.

She couldn't stand it any longer. The anticipation was killing her and I could see it as she leaned in closer. She was sitting on the very edge of her seat and her legs were bouncing with antsy anticipation.

"Tell me!" she exclaimed.

"Okay. You ready? You, my friend, are going to call yourself 'Avril and The Tuques'."

I laughed. She laughed, partially because she thought it was funny, but probably more so because she was relieved to know that I wasn't serious.

I guess in my own way, despite not having the wisdom to know it at the time, what I was really saying in that joke was, "Your name really doesn't matter that much. The music matters. Call yourself whatever you want. But don't spend too much time thinking about it."

For the rest of the night, Avril smiled and shook hands with all the industry execs that had come to meet her -- I could tell she'd rather be anywhere else, though. If she could just sneak away and write a song, or work on a logo, or write even one lyrical couplet -- any of it would be better than a smoke-clouded New York bar filled with industry executives.

That night strengthened my belief that Avril would be a star. She did what she needed to do, despite not wanting to do it. More importantly, she trusted the business people around her -- her manager and her potential new A&R rep -- so when they said, "We need to go meet a bunch of industry people," she did what needed to be done. All she really wanted to do was write a song and figure out, in her own mind, whether she would be known as Avril or Avril Lavigne. Ironically, years and millions and millions of albums later, it didn't matter. She started as Avril Lavigne, but became so incredibly popular, everyone knows who you mean when you refer to just "Avril."

I still think she should have been Avril and the Tuques. No I don't. But it was a fun thought at the moment.

Avril and I, sporting our tuques, during one of her co-writing trips in New York.

Sex and Candy

I discovered the hit song "Sex & Candy" by Marcy Playground. Well, sort of. That song would have done just fine with or without me, but I might have just nudged it along a little.

In 1995 my college friend Andy and I had no intentions of making a living in the music business. Honestly, I didn't even consider it as an option, particularly living in Raleigh, North Carolina. Sure, I had dreams of maybe making it as a musician, but even that was quite the stretch if I were to have been perfectly honest with myself.

We decided to put out a compilation CD of songs that we just really liked. We didn't care about success, or it being anything ground breaking. We just wanted to put out a CD of great songs by great bands. And when I say "put out," we had no earthly idea how to actually get a CD in the stores. Remember, this was long before the Internet explosion that made music distribution easy.

One night at a show at The Cat's Cradle in Chapel Hill, North Carolina we met a guy named Tor Hansen. We told him about our idea of putting out a CD, and he mentioned to us that he had started a distribution company and that he could possibly get our CD into stores. We later met with Tor and he had 3 photocopied pieces of paper showing us his entire distribution catalog. It may have only been 2 pages... he didn't have very many titles. Still, it was the closest thing we knew to distribution at the time, so we agreed to have our CD run through his company, which by the way was (and is) called Redeye Distribution. They have since won all sorts of awards as an independent distributor.

Distribution was in place. For all we knew, he might get it in 3 stores or he might get it in 3000. We didn't really know, or care. We had distribution. Now we just needed to get this CD done.

We had already signed a dozen or so great acts for our first CD including Butch Walker's project at the time, The Floyds. Also signed were Athenaeum (who eventually went on to big success with an album on Atlantic), Donna The Buffalo, All Mighty Senators, Uncle Mingo, and a few other well-known regional touring acts. We were coming close to having what we believed was a CD filled with great songs by great musicians.

Andy had a friend who worked at EMI Records. His friend wasn't very high up on the corporate ladder, but he was probably the biggest person we knew personally in the business. His friend used to send us boxes of cassette tapes of "rejected demos," or sometimes he'd send us samplers of new acts they had signed and were planning to release. We always enjoyed weeding through those boxes of demos. In some way, I guess it was teaching us which acts were of the caliber of a major label and which ones were not.

We decided to go visit our friend at EMI in New York one

weekend. We certainly didn't have the money to fly, so we set out to drive it in Andy's black Nissan Altima. In the car with us was a care package of rejected demo tapes from EMI. Starting in North Carolina heading North on I-95, we popped in one tape after another, listening to anything and everything. There were probably 100 tapes total in that box.

And remember, we were only listening to these for fun. We thought it was cool to get to hear all this different music from around the country. Again, keep in mind this was before the Internet made it easy to listen to music from around the world. Getting to hear a random band (even a bad band) from Topeka, Kansas was not something just anyone could do.

Around the time we hit the New Jersey turnpike, I pulled out of the box a tape by a band called Marcy Playground. We had already listened to about 80 tapes, most of which were horrible. On this one was a note from our friend saying they had signed these guys a while back but that he didn't think EMI was going to release it. Within minutes of listening I remember saying,

"Oh my God! Listen to this, Andy!"

Andy either has ADD or is just a great multi-tasker. He is the only guy I know that can talk on his cell phone, read a road map, drive, carry on a conversation with a person inside the car, and change his clothes all at the same time. So when he doesn't hear what I'm hearing with the Marcy Playground tape, I can't really blame him. He was solving world hunger and navigating a faster route through New Jersey all at the same time. And to top it off, this was about our 80th tape of the day. So after my "Oh God!" outburst, I recall Andy saying, while reading a road map and checking his pager, something along the lines of, "What? What's wrong? Is it bad?"

"Hell no. It's brilliant. This is the best music I've heard in years," I exclaimed.

We listened to that entire album.

When we arrived in New York I became very inquisitive about this band Marcy Playground. Our friend at EMI told me about how there were no plans in place to release the record.

Honestly, I didn't really care about the band's story. I was just happy to have some great new music to listen to. We listened to it over and over again on the ride back to North Carolina. I couldn't get those infectious songs out of my head. A month or so went by and I continued to listen to this Marcy Playground tape, playing it for anyone who cared to listen, even some that probably didn't.

By this time we had rounded out most of the track listing to complete our first CD. We had room for one more song. Andy and I were planning to head back to New York for another visit and to go to some shows. I said to him, "Why don't we ask EMI if they'd let us put Marcy Playground on our CD?"

So we made some calls and our friend arranged for us to meet with the A&R Rep who had originally signed the band. I was a nervous wreck. I had never met with an A&R Rep. Hell, I didn't even know what "A&R" stood for. What would I say to such royalty of the music business? What should I wear? All I could think about was this big meeting to ask if I could put a song by Marcy Playground on our CD.

Our time came. We waited in the lobby of the magnificent EMI Records in New York City and out came the assistant to the A&R rep. "He'll see you now," she said, while signaling for us to follow her.

As we entered the A&R rep's office, he said in a thick New York accent, "So, I hear you're doing a compilation CD and you want to put a Marcy Playground song on there."

"Why? And what song?" he continued.... And here's where it gets a little fuzzy in my mind. After all, I was a nervous wreck, in a New York record label office, with no intentions of making a living in the music business, and certainly no intentions of one day writing it all down in a book. But to my best recollection, Mr. A&R said something along the lines of the reason they weren't sure about putting out the album was because they were uncertain about a single. So he wanted to know why I would want to release a song by a band who potentially had no hit single, and if so, which song would I want to release.

"I dunno," I shrugged. "I just like their music."

"And what song would you want?" he pressed.

Again, I think I shrugged and answered with some poetic and business-like response, "I dunno. Any song is fine by me. I like 'em all."

In my mind, I knew the song I wanted. I wasn't lying, I did like them all. But I knew I wanted "Sex & Candy," but I didn't want to *not* get a Marcy Playground song just because I picked the wrong song. I felt like I was on some game show where if I said the wrong song he'd hit a big buzzer and the floor would open up and I'd go hurtling down a corridor to the dungeon of losers who can't pick a good song. So I spoke softly and cautiously and said, "I kinda like that song 'Sex & Candy'."

"Really?" he responded. And again, in my fuzzy memory I believe he followed that by telling me *that* song was definitely not the single.

"Yeah, I like that song. But any song would be fine. But sure, 'Sex and Candy' would be great."

"Okay, send me a contract," he said.

And just like that, my meeting with the A&R God was over in less than 5 minutes.

So we sent him a contract, they signed it, and we became the first record company to release "Sex & Candy." When our CD (*Deep Volume I*) finally came out, that song started to get some really good buzz in the college radio and underground independent music scene.

Eventually, EMI put out the Marcy Playground album. I'd like to think it was because of the buzz we created for it, and maybe it was, but it all happened primarily because that was a brilliant song.

It wasn't smooth sailing for Marcy Playground from there. EMI didn't have success with their album. They put it out, but nothing happened. And shortly after, Capital Records acquired their catalog and re-released the same album, and they were the label to eventually put the song to #1 on the charts.

"Sex and Candy" then spent a record-breaking 15 weeks at #1 on the Billboard Modern Rock charts, beating out Oasis' "Wonderwall" which spent 10 weeks in the top position.

Still to this day, I consider John Wozniak (singer/songwriter for Marcy Playground) to be one of the greatest songwriters of recent times. And if you ask him, he'll tell you I played a role in him having a career in music. But really, it came down to the fact that "Sex & Candy" is an undeniably brilliant song.

Me, John Wozniak and Dylan Keefe (Marcy Playground)

Had I not discovered it, someone else would have. And they, like me, would have told everyone they came in contact with that this is incredible music.

From the day I heard "Sex & Candy" to the time it hit #1 on the pop charts was almost 2 years.

Great music doesn't always immediately find its way to the right ears, but it eventually almost always does. Have patience and believe in the songs you know to be brilliant. If you're right, time will tell.

Are record labels dead?

There has never been a better time in the history of the music industry to be a musician. The barrier-to-entry is relatively low. On the downside, it means more people have entered the field.

Back when I was in high school and college (late '80s / early '90s), it was rare to know someone in a band. Now, it's rare if you *don't* know someone in a band. Everybody has a band these days.

The good news is it's easier than ever to get your music recorded and heard. The bad news is there's more music out there than ever before to compete with.

There was a time when the only path to success was to catch the attention of a record label. Thankfully, not anymore. Now, anyone with a recorded song can have worldwide distribution and immediate access to millions and millions of possible music fans.

The thing that hasn't changed much is the fact that you still need great music to rise to the top. Prior to the Internet age, record labels decided which bands were worthy of being heard by the masses. Today, the public can decide what is great without the assistance of record labels.

The problem is, there are so many options available to the public that we music fans need a filter. We still need someone to help us weed through all the crap. Sometimes that can be a high number of views on an Internet video channel, or maybe it's a huge number of fans on a social media site. Just because you have a great song and you've put it on the Internet, does not mean people will magically find it -- you need to market through the immense number of available outlets. Today it's Facebook, Twitter, YouTube, ReverbNation, and dozens of others. Tomorrow it will be something else. Nevertheless, the concept remains the same: utilize filter outlets to help your music get heard.

Fortunately, you are no longer in need of a record label to determine your fate. You determine your own fate. Again though, you *must* have great music. Without that, no amount of marketing is going to force the public to like your songs.

So why go with a record label? Record labels aren't dead yet. They're just different. Look at a record label as an additional marketing arm for your team. They can help you get on the radio if you're the type of artist that would be played on the radio. And they usually have money that can help advertise your music.

At one time in the industry, the only way to get your music heard was to allow a record label to own your recordings. But now record labels are often your partners. A great record label can be a huge asset to your career. Fortunately, you no longer need to wait for their approval to get your music noticed.

A fair deal with a reputable record label can be an amazing asset to your career. Look at a good record label as another member of your team.

Yes, all the marketing amenities once only offered to record labels are now at the fingertips of everyone, which makes for a more level playing field, but the right record label can be your partner in helping grow your career.

There was a time when artists would get signed to a record label and have this sense of, "Whew. My work is finally over. I can play and have fun. The label will now do all of the work." Those days are gone. A good record label should work *with* you, not *for* you.

Q: *Levi from Austin, TX asks: How do I get my song in front of and listened to by a program director?*

A: Not many commercial radio stations play local music. Some do, but not many. And those who do usually play it because the buzz about you is so big in town, the program director has heard about you from dozens and dozens of different sources. If the program director is hearing about you for the first time *from* you, it's unlikely that all the conversations in the world will cause them to play your music.

My suggestion is to create a buzz. Build a big local fan base. Build a loyal fan base. Do this, and program directors will find you, if it fits their station.

But by all means, please don't ask your 20 friends to call the radio station and request your music. All radio stations have seen this game hundreds of times and they can see right through it. Even U2 doesn't get requested 20 times a day. So if your 20 friends are calling to request your music, you have just drastically decreased your chances of ever being played on that station.

Don't hang your career on getting your music heard by a program director. Yes, a program director of a great station can absolutely help kick-start the career of a band, but it must happen naturally. Forced "sales pitches" on program directors never work.

That said, if you're dead set on meeting with the program director, my suggestion is to start by supporting the station. That starts with listening regularly. Then, go support some of their remote broadcasts. Are they broadcasting live from an auto parts store near you? This is probably a good time to go buy that new oil filter you have needed to buy. While there, introduce yourself to the DJ that is broadcasting. Don't interrupt their work, just politely introduce yourself. And don't hand them your demo. Get to know them. It's okay to tell them about your band or invite them to a show, but don't stalk them by showing up wearing your band T-shirt and handing them your latest recording.

Continue to support the station long term. Develop a relationship with the station. Get involved in charities they support. Get involved in community functions they support. And eventually, you'll get to know them. Remember, they broadcast to *your* community, so they want to get to know the members of that community.

Approach radio people just like you would anyone. Be friendly, but not overbearing.

Once you've developed a good rapport with the staff, perhaps offer to perform for free at one of their functions or events, asking nothing in return.

Continue to support that station, and they'll likely want to support you.

With that said no amount of friendship, rapport, or community support makes up for bad music. Make sure your music is damn good. The radio is the top of the ladder for quality songs and recordings, so you'd better have a recording that lives up to those standards.

It's unlikely a cold-call is going to get you in to meet with a program director. Take it slow. Support the station and eventually you'll get there. In the meantime, continue building your local fan base to be loyal and large.

The A&R rep

"Damnit!" That's the reaction most artists would have if a record company guy left after seeing only 10 minutes of their show. And it's the wrong reaction.

When I was in the hair-band Paris Red, around 1990, we got an opening slot for Jackyl. A guy by the name of Cliff Witherspoon was working with Jackyl. He saw our set and liked it, and in many ways took us under his wing. He was the biggest guy I knew in the music business at the time. Jackyl was signed to Geffen Records by the famed A&R rep John Kalodner. So that was big... more like HUGE, to my little band from Raleigh, North Carolina, to have someone in that camp rooting for us.

Andy Martin and I were managing the various bands I was in prior to us starting Deep South Records. Although we didn't consciously know it at the time, we were learning the business at the expense of my bands. Not a literal financial expense, but we were just learning how to navigate the music business using my bands as the vehicle. For the first several years of Deep South, I was both a musician in a band signed to Deep South *and* the label co-owner.

Andy and I loved music, and the business that surrounded it. We'd sit up for hours talking about different aspects of the business -- mostly trying to figure out how to "break" my band into the big time. Little did we know, all this preparation was setting us up for a more successful path ahead in starting a label.

83

One night at about 2 am in the spring of 1995, we were talking on the phone. I don't recall who said it first, but one of us said, "We should just do it. Let's just start a record label."

In the words of Steve Jobs, "Sometimes not knowing what you're up against is a good thing." That was us.

Andy and I had been managing my various bands for about 7 years at this point. We had learned a lot, but we were just getting started.

At the time when we started Deep South Records, the big scam in the music business was "pay to play" compilation CDs. Shyster "record labels" would promise bands to get their music heard by the bigwigs at major labels by putting them on a compilation CD. The only hook was the bands had to pay to be on these compilations -- sometimes really big money. And if you wanted to be the first or second song on the CD, you had to pay more. It was a huge scam in the mid-90s. And as a result, there was some seriously cringe worthy music on most of these compilation CDs. Labels didn't listen to them because they were just not good. What label wants to listen to a band just because their daddies had the $600 it cost to put them on the CD?

When we started Deep South, our grand business plan was to do a compilation CD, only different. We thought, "What if we didn't charge the bands anything? Not a dime. What if we just pick great music and put in on the CD?" We figured labels would pay attention knowing that not a single band paid to be on the compilation. And the labels did pay attention. 17 bands from our first 3 CDs went on to get major label record deals. We had hit on something unique.

Don't go giving me a "Way to go there, Dave" pat on the back just yet. Our motives weren't completely pure. Yes, we were committed to putting great music on our compilations, and we were committed to none of the bands paying to be included. We would seek out the "hot" bands in major markets. Back then there was no Google. You couldn't look on MySpace or Facebook to see how many "friends" or "likes" a band had. So we would call local record stores in various cities and ask, "What local band is selling well?" We would also call local college stations and local newspapers and ask about the buzzing band in the area.

We would find the best music we could possibly find in different cities, mostly around the southeast, but the catch was that we'd put my band on those CDs as well. At the time my band was called 9811. We were a 3-piece indie pop rock band with a few catchy little songs, but by no means were we the "buzz" band. So our plan was to do a compilation CD of great music, filled with all these   buzz   bands from major markets, and stick 9811 right in the middle.

For one, it would be easier for 9811 to get gigs in the venues in these markets. Venue owners would look at the compilation and check off 6 or 8 acts on the CD that were already selling out their room. And when we would call and say, "Could we book 9811 in your room? They're on the same compilation with {insert names of popular regional bands here}," we would surely get the gigs.   And we did. Unfortunately we didn't have the undeniably brilliant music to sustain us, but it got our foot in the door.

So now came the hard part -- finding the brilliant music. No Google. No ReverbNation. No Facebook. No YouTube where we could just log on and see live clips of bands. We had to actually get in our car and drive to hear bands live. And boy did we. From New York to Nashville to Florida and everywhere in between we would drive to go hear a band we had learned about from some record store or local radio station.

When you're starting a label and don't really know anyone in the business, you basically try to network with anyone and everyone you can.

I had stayed in touch with Cliff Witherspoon (the Jackyl guy) over the years. He told me about a couple of bands he was managing in Atlanta that were really "buzzing." So Andy and I hopped in the car and drove to Atlanta for the weekend to check these bands out. To date, we had not signed anyone to Deep South. This was one of our first road trips as a label.

Let me back up a bit. It is kind of funny looking back on it... after

Andy and I had our big, "Yeah, let's do this, let's start a record label" moment, and after the high-fives died down.... reality set in and at some point in that conversation we said, "Okay. What do you think we should do first?"

I think it was me that said, "I guess we should print up some business cards, and we should probably get a phone line installed so that we can answer the phone 'Deep South Records' and sound official. Yeah, that will make us a real record label." Or so we thought.

So we did. We printed business cards. We had a separate phone line installed in my apartment, complete with a cassette tape answering machine.

Back to Atlanta... We went down to Atlanta to check out these bands our friend Cliff was working on. While in the motel room we were reading through the weekly entertainment paper, Creative Loafing. We would *always* pick up the weekly entertainment paper anywhere we went. It was our way to follow the trends of music, the new venues, and who was playing where.

As I was browsing through this issue, partially confirming the addresses of the venues we were planning to visit that night, and partially just seeing what else was going on, I saw a listing for a band called Floyds Funk Revival playing at Smith's Olde Bar.

I said to Andy, "Floyds Funk Revival. Hey, I think that band has members in it from the band SouthGang." SouthGang was a hair band in 1990 that had very little success. But being a former hair-band guy myself, I knew everything there was to know about hair-bands, as did Andy.

We had a packed schedule of bands we were planning to go see that night, but just for fun, we decided we'd stop in to Smith's to see this band Floyds Funk Revival, which we assumed would just be made up of old washed-up hair-band guys. But it would be cool to us. We loved everything about hair-bands, so we were really curious to see what this was all about. Most hair-bands just dried up and blew away by 1995, so to hear about guys still doing it, under another name, was pretty intriguing. Maybe they'd even play an old

SouthGang song.

We didn't have a lot of money then. We couldn't even afford the cover charges to get in to see all these bands we wanted to catch. We'd have to smooth-talk our way in. Back in 1995, flashing a business card for a record label actually carried some weight. I don't really know why. Anyone could get business cards printed for $9.95 at Office Depot. But it worked. That cheap-ass Deep South business card somehow got us in for free to see Floyds Funk Revival.

We didn't really know our way around Atlanta, and this was obviously way before GPS, so we called a couple of old friends we knew in town to hang out with us on our "scouting" excursion. They weren't really close friends. I don't even remember their names. But they knew the city and were willing to drive us around, so we let them tag along in exchange for them being our tour guides. They were more the "dance club" type folks, I do remember that, so their idea of going to see a bunch of bands wasn't very exciting, but we promised them we'd end up at a dance club at the end of the night.

Floyds Funk Revival featured Butch Walker as the singer. Butch was the guitar player in SouthGang.

If you don't know who Butch is, learn everything you can about him. He's produced and written for some of the biggest artists in the world, and he's a brilliant artist as well. Seriously, if you're an aspiring musician - and I can only assume you are if you're reading this book - then look up Butch Walker and study his career.

I was absolutely blown away. Floored. Seeing Butch Walker own that stage at Smith's Olde Bar was unlike anything I had ever seen in my life. I still don't think I've ever seen someone own a stage like Butch does.

We were there only 10 minutes. I had only heard 2 songs from Floyds Funk Revival when I turned to Andy and said, "Come on. Let's go. We've got a lot of bands to see tonight."

One of our dance-club friends said to me, as to agree with my suggestion for a quick exit "Yeah, these guys are lame. Good call. Let's get out of here."

"Lame?" I said. "Are you kidding me? This is freakin' brilliant. Probably the best I've ever seen or heard."

On my way out, I went over to the merchandise table and met Butch's dad. I gave him my freshly printed Deep South Records business card and over the loud music said to him something along the lines of, "I absolutely love this band and would like to talk more. Here's my card."

So we left. We only stayed 10 minutes. But that was all I needed. I knew this guy was going to be one of the biggest stars in the world. I was right.

We had returned to Raleigh by Monday after that fast weekend in Atlanta. I remember sitting in my apartment, probably watching Law & Order re-runs, and I heard this strange ring that I had never heard before. It sounded like a phone, but it wasn't the phone ring I was accustomed to hearing. I turned the volume down on the TV to listen more closely and then it hit me: *Oh shit. That's the Deep South Records phone we had just installed.* It had never rung before, of course.

I rushed to the phone. I cleared my throat as to sound professional. Who could be our very first call to Deep South Records? Surely it was just a telemarketer.

"Deep South Records," I said as I answered our label phone for the very first time.

"Hi. This is Butch Walker. Is Dave Rose there?"

Holy cow! Butch Walker is calling me.

Butch said, "I got your card that you left us at our show this weekend...."

Butch and I talked for about 15 minutes. I told him about the compilation CD we were doing and he agreed to be on it. We sent him our homemade record contract the very next day and he returned it, signed, within a week.

Our very first executed record contract, and with Butch Walker, no less.

Deep South went on to feature Butch's projects on future compilations: The Floyds, and then The Marvelous 3 with their hit song, "Freak of the Week." The Marvelous 3 would go on to sign to Elektra Records.

I'd like to think we played a role in the success of Butch Walker's career. Andy ended up getting Butch his first co-write session with SR-71 (co-writing the hit "Miss Right Now"), that ultimately lead to a long string of co-writes for Butch.

But truthfully, with or without Deep South, Butch would have been just fine because he writes undeniably brilliant songs. And when you have undeniably brilliant music, your cousin Rick will surely tell everyone he knows about that music.

Butch is incredibly talented. And he has spent thousands of hours honing his skills. Butch Walker would have become Butch Walker just fine without little old Deep South. But it feels good having been there in the beginning to recognize his talent and share that talent, and music, with others.

Butch and I became pretty good friends over the years. I don't stay in touch with him like I should, but he's always been a huge influence on me, and not just musically speaking. He's a good guy with grounded morals. He's a "do the right thing" kind of guy with an amazing work ethic, and I'd like to think he sensed the same out of Andy and me.

I'm very thankful to Butch for taking a chance with such a small company as Deep South. To this day, he's still one of my favorite people in the business.

In all the times Butch stayed at my house when he was touring with The Floyds and The Marvelous 3, I don't believe I ever told him this story.

The lesson here for you: Just because a music industry person leaves your show after 2 songs, that's not necessarily a bad thing. Two songs were all I needed to realize that Butch Walker was a star.

Q: *Vincent from Miami, FL asks: How can you score a meeting with a label rep?*

A: Make undeniably brilliant music and you'll get more meetings than you could ever imagine. And P.S. Don't use the word "score." It makes you sound like a tool. Don't worry about getting a meeting. Worry about making music that people tell people about. If you give your song to 100 people and none of them pass it along to their friends, all the label meetings in the world won't make your life better.

Just make great music and I promise the meetings will come to you. If the meetings aren't coming to you, you're probably not as good as you need to be.

We need a manager

That's a very common phrase I hear from local bands. Just so we're clear, a manager is the person who oversees and directs all aspects of your career. A booking agent is typically under the direction of the manager. A booking agent is responsible for booking shows and tours.

Usually when a local band says "We need a manager," what they are really hoping for is a booking agent. Getting a great booking agent is a huge catch-22. You can't get a great agent until you can prove you don't need an agent.

Concentrate on building your local fan base then expand into other markets. If you get to the point where you are selling out several venues in several cities, it's likely that a great booking agent will find you. Booking agents talk to venues all the time. Word travels fast if you're selling out half-a-dozen venues within a 200-mile radius.

Almost every city has a few good local and regional booking agents. I recommend getting to know them, or at least send them regular updates as to what's happening with your band. If you just played three sold out shows, send them an email letting them know.

Yes, eventually you will need a great booking agent and even a manager. But your first priority needs to be proving that you don't need either. Once you can do that, they (and many other industry professionals) will come knocking.

Q: Reggie from Washington, D.C. asks: If a music manager, publisher, plugger or booking agent tells you that they can submit you as an artist or your material to other artists for a monthly fee until something happens, is it worth it?

A: In my 20 years in the music business, I've never taken on an artist for a fee. It's not to say that I wouldn't, or that it's necessarily a bad thing, I just never have.

A manager, a publisher, a plugger, and a booking agent all have very different roles and different ways of making money. So to lump them all into the same category is unfair.

It's not unheard of for a manager or booking agent to take on a young new artist on retainer. Typically a manager or booking agent makes money by earning a percentage of the artist's earnings. In the beginning, that artist doesn't earn money. So sometimes the manager or agent will charge a fee to work that artist.

Do not pay a publisher. A publisher is in the business of retaining rights, either copyrights or administrative rights, to your songs. Paying them up front is not common. I'd be skeptical of this sort of business relationship.

Song pluggers: maybe. Yes, many song pluggers will take on new writers for a fee. There are entire companies whose business models are to accept money to listen to your songs, and should one be good enough, pitch it to others.

As with anything, do your homework on the company or individual in question. Talk to people who have worked with these companies. If they've had good results, then likely you are entering into a good situation.

Generally speaking, whenever possible, avoid paying anyone up front who typically works on commission or would retain rights to your music.

For example, publicists do not typically work on commission nor do they retain rights to your works, therefore it's normal to pay an upfront fee when hiring a publicist.

But it's not unheard of, nor is it necessarily unethical for a manager, agent or plugger to accept a fee for their work. You just need to *really* do your homework before agreeing to work with them; otherwise you may be throwing your money away.

> *Cousin Rick says:* Improve your email list this week, either by making signup more available online or by offering "free stuff" when people sign up at a show. Your email list is your most valuable asset to help grow your fan base, and thus get an agent or manager.

All for one and one for all?

Only in fairy tales like *The Three Musketeers* may that philosophy apply. Rarely does it apply in bands.

When I tell musicians who are interested in a career in popular music that he or she needs to lose some weight, they are often quick to reference examples like Meatloaf or John Popper (of Blues Traveler). "There are big guys who have made it big. Look at Meatloaf!" They love to rebut as if it justifies their own weight issues.

Name me five overweight popular singers and I'll name you 50,000 physically fit ones. I'm not here to get into the sociological or psychological reasons as to why that is — it just is what it is. Popular music fans like their musicians physically fit for the most part, but out-of-shape musicians love to point out the exceptions to the rule. Yes, there are exceptions to *every* rule in music, but if you're trying to break into a business that is already hard enough to break, I'm just telling you how to beat the odds.

So when I share with you what I'm about to share with you, please don't write me pointing out exceptions to the rule. I'm sure there are exceptions, but what I'm about to tell you is generally true among most successful bands.

A band cannot be a democracy. You need a leader.

I'm not necessarily suggesting the leader needs to make more money than the others, I'm mostly just pointing out that a band needs a definitive voice. In any given day, particularly for a successful band, there are literally hundreds of decisions that a band must make. Yes, you will have a manager guiding many of those decisions, but still that manager will need someone within the band with whom to discuss these topics.

Sure, in the early stages, when a band has maybe three decisions a week to make, it's easy to be a democracy. Do we take the gig at Joe's Pub or not? Do we make a video for this song or that song? It is easy when there is very little at stake and there are very few decisions to be made. If you make decisions as a democracy and screw it up as a young band, who cares? It is all part of the learning process. You still have your day job, thankfully, and you would probably not put your career in jeopardy if you screw up a Joe's Pub gig in the early stages of the band.

But to avoid future conflict, appoint a band leader early on in your career and stand behind the decisions that leader makes.

This is not to say you hand over all the work to one person. Duties should be split among band members according to their respective talents, but one of you needs to be the voice of the band, the decision maker.

Naturally, this person is often one who is key to the musical dynamic of the band; the singer or the songwriter. Consider this: if you are a band and one person writes and sings the majority of the songs, then without that person are you really the same band? Probably not. So, it would be natural for that person to be the decision maker in the band.

Most mega-million selling bands have one leader, but some presumably have two: Keith Richards and Mick Jagger. Joe Perry and Steven Tyler. Paul McCartney and John Lennon. Bono and The Edge. But more often than not, and I would argue even in these four cases, one person has the final say.

Aside from it being impossible time-wise for four or five band members to come to an agreement on hundreds of decisions daily, it just doesn't make sense for the structure of the business. Would a bank or a major tech company be successful if the CEO gathered his or her staff for every single decision? No, of course not. They would spend their entire day deciding every little detail of the business. There is one leader who makes the big decisions and delegates tasks to his co-workers. Appoint a "CEO" among your bandmates to lead.

It *must* be this way in a successful band. Remember, your band is a business. So who is the tech geek in the band? That person is responsible for websites and social media sites. Who is the artsy one? That person should be in charge of graphics, logos, set designs. Maybe you have a finance-minded person in the band who can keep your books and tax records. However, one of you, and it doesn't matter who it is, needs to be the leader -- the final decision maker.

Do you hire this booking agent or another one? Do you fire your drum tech? What is the best way to spend the money? Should your album be released in the summer or the fall? What should be the title of the next album? Should you take the day off between Portland and Reno, or try to fill the date between the two? Do you do the interview with Spin or Rolling Stone? Or Both?

I could go on for days with the gazillions of decisions that need to be made on a daily basis with successful bands.

There is a difference between a leader and a dictator. Good leaders surround themselves with smart people, some of whom are often in the same band. Leaders should seek advice, input, and wisdom from those around them. A good leader will always look to others for wisdom. However, a good leader will also be decisive and confident, knowing that even if he makes the wrong decision he will have the support of his team, and he will realize his mistakes and correct those mistakes.

A good leader motivates the team. A good leader wakes up early, works hard, and is in constant communication with those on the team.

Many times a band does not officially appoint a leader because it becomes apparent early on who the natural leader is. But, regardless of whether this comes naturally or not to your band, it is something you need to discuss. The longer you wait, the harder it will get. Start your leader in training early on in your band's career because you certainly don't want that leader "learning the ropes" when major decisions are at play. Let him screw up a $100 gig at Joe's Pub. Let him forget to order band merchandise for the upcoming weekend tour you have. Let him forget to spell-check the liner notes in the CD. Leaders need to make some mistakes so that down the road when much more is at stake, he or she will have learned from the mistakes.

Who is that person in your band? Choose your leader and stand behind the leader's decisions. Offer your wisdom and support in your areas of expertise. Trust this person to make sound decisions on behalf of your band. Get your leader started early and encourage him as he grows, as he makes mistakes, and as he learns to strengthen your business from those mistakes.

All for one and one for all is great for fairy tales. But it's not the way it works in the real world of bands.

Cousin Rick says: Are you in a band? Talk about this topic in a band meeting this week. Start the discussions of picking a band leader if you do not have one already.

Q: *Sade from Brooklyn, NY asks: When is it a good idea to play for free or less than our normal guarantee?*

A: There are a lot of reasons to play for free or for less than what you normally make. Perhaps there's a charity that's dear to you. Support them by playing at one of their events. Or maybe you regularly play X venue and you'd prefer to be playing Y venue. If Y venue calls with an amazing opening slot for a band whose fans would probably like your music, then don't worry about the money. Play. Or maybe a city festival can put you in front of 10,000 new people with loads of radio and print exposure leading up to the event. Don't worry about the money. Play.

As a rising artist, there are not many cases where money should be your primary concern. Develop the fans. Play the right rooms. Get in front of the right crowds. Seek out events that will get your name out to a new audience. If you're good enough, the money will fall in place at the right time.

Q: *Carter from Detroit, MI asks: If you submit a song to a music publisher with just a handshake, and no one puts a hold on it or cuts the tune, what happens to that song? Can you still submit it to other publishers?*

A: Absolutely. Just be sure to communicate your intentions with the owner of the hand that you shook. Believe it or not, there's not really that many hands in the business and they all know each other. So if you shake a hand on a deal, stand behind your bond.

However, submitting a song to a publisher is just that, a submission. Until that publisher decides to do something with it, and assuming you don't have a deal in place, then that song is yours to do with what you want. But like I say, communicate everything. If you're honest with everyone in advance, you will not burn bridges.

Demystifying the press kit

The first thing you need to include in your press kit is a photo of yourself on a railroad track. In front of a brick wall will do equally as well, though.

I'm kidding.

There are several things to consider in a good press kit. For those of you wondering, you do *not* need a physical press kit. Don't waste your money.

1. Put everything online. Sites like ReverbNation are great, but you can also build your own press website.

2. Don't give me too much information. I don't want to know what your favorite color is, and honestly, I don't even care what kind of guitar you play. Leave out the fluff.

3. Include good pictures. Give me some good promo shots and some good live shots, but don't include 50 pictures. 5 or 10 will do. I don't want to see pictures of you downing Jagerbombs with your friends at a sports bar.

4. Make a good video. A video is important. But not one your dad shot holding a camcorder while talking to your mom and all I can hear is dad saying, "Look at Johnny play. I'm so proud of him." Give me a good video. Videos are relatively inexpensive to make these days. People listen with their eyes. Follow the stats on any band website and you will see that video views usually bring the most hits.

5. Include music. Not your catalog and garage recordings in their entirety; give me just enough music to make me want more.

6. Write a bio. Once again, leave out the fluff. Yes, cover some of the basics, like where you are from, recent and relevant accomplishments, immediate plans (and don't say "We're gonna be the next Beatles"), just a story of some sort. Did your band relocate to Nashville from Sweden? Was your singer the guy in the Chili's commercial? Do all of the members of the band work day jobs as lumberjacks? Any of that stuff makes for a good story. Give it to me. You've got a story of your own. Include it in your bio. And by the way, "We all met in high school and our diverse musical backgrounds have fused together to create a sound never before heard".... Well, that story we've heard a gazillion times. Come up with something better than that.

7. Quote relevant folks. Give me a few quotes from people who matter. Is there a venue where you're bringing great attendance? Get a quote from the venue owner. Has your material received favorable reviews from a reputable blog or magazine? Include a quote from that publication. Again, no fluff. If you only have two good quotes from two reputable sources, just include those.

8. Include your contact information. Don't get me interested in your music only to make it difficult for me to contact you. Make contacting you easy. A valid email address and phone number are essential.

Q: *Alan from Boston, MA asks: Should I copyright my songs?*

A: I believe you mean to ask, "Should I *register* my songs with the United States Copyright Office?" because technically your songs are already copyrighted when you write them. Once you write your song down or record it, your song is in fact copyrighted. Registering these songs is just one method of proving these songs are yours. It's currently $35 to register each song or a collection of songs. As you've read in my book, you will possibly need to write hundreds of songs before seeing a career in music. At bare minimum you will likely write several dozen. This could get expensive, and possibly unnecessarily so.

That said, in all my years in the business, I've never known of someone stealing a song, ever. Furthermore, careers are made from multiple songs, not one single song. So if you're lucky enough to write a song that someone steals and turns into a hit, not only will you be the first case I've ever seen of this happening, you likely have 50 more where those came from. Consider yourself blessed that you possess the ability to write a successful song and know that you are able to write more.

I'm not suggesting you leave your car unlocked for anyone to rummage through and steal your belongings, I just don't want you to worry about the wrong things. Worry about how to write a great song first. And know that you're more likely to get struck by lightning four times in the same day than you are to have your song stolen.

Most cases of copyright infringement are high-profile cases where people claim a big artist has stolen their song. I would venture to say most of these claims are frivolous and hold very little merit. Yes, there probably are documented cases of songs being legitimately stolen, it's just extremely uncommon.

My suggestion is to keep good records of the songs you write. Demo and record as many as you can, mostly for creative reasons, but also so that you can have good proof that you wrote the song should it ever come to question. Again, it's unlikely it ever will. But rather than spending a bunch of money registering your first 100 songs, I'd prefer you spend that time and effort refining your craft. If lightning ever does strike you four times in one day, consider yourself lucky – you, my friend, know how to write a great song and are one of the few. In which case, go write some more and build a career off of that.

Do we need a lawyer?

Maybe. It just depends on where you are in your career. When you are just starting out, you probably don't need a lawyer. But once your business starts to become more established and more deals start crossing your plate, you will absolutely want to get a good attorney involved.

They can be expensive, but the money they cost you in the short run will more than pay for itself down the road. A good lawyer will structure a fair deal that will bring you financial rewards in the long run, as well as help to protect you from bad deals.

I recommend attorneys who are familiar with the music business. The music business is a unique animal, so your dad's tax attorney may not be the right guy to handle a record contract from an independent label that has offered to put your song on a compilation CD.

The most common mistake I see local bands make on this topic is getting a lawyer involved *too* soon. Before they've even played their first gig or put out their first CD, they've hired a lawyer to incorporate their band, copyright register their songs, and create a forty-page band partnership agreement.

Write a great song first. Or better yet, write fifty great songs first. Play out for a while. Build a fan base. And once you get some momentum going, get an attorney involved to help you navigate the legal aspect of your career. But don't break the bank hiring an attorney before you've even written your first dozen songs.

When your band is just starting, it's important for you to keep good records of your finances. As with the attorney, you don't need to hire an accountant right out of the gate. But you do need to keep good records. I recommend getting an accountant involved after you've been an organization (a band) for about a year. In that first year, do it yourself.

Open a checking account to keep your band's money separate. It doesn't even need to be a fancy corporate account. You can open an inexpensive joint checking account with your other band mates. More than likely there will not be much incoming money your first year of business, so you should be able to track it well yourself. It's no different than managing your own personal checking account.

You do need to keep track of the money you are earning and spending for tax purposes. And again, once you've been in operation for about a year, a good accountant can advise you on the tax laws in your area, and help you prepare for proper tax reporting.

Q: Natasia from Sacramento, CA asks: Before I collaborate with other musicians on an original song project, should I get something in writing first?

A: Getting things in writing is always helpful but don't let it stand in the way of the creative process.

It's good to discuss things like: How do you plan on splitting the songwriting, percentage-wise? If you record, who owns the recordings?

Although getting things in writing is good, I caution artists to not get too caught up in the legalese of the music business before they even create a great product. Cover the basics up front, but don't be afraid to dive right in to making great music when the opportunity strikes.

I once received a phone call from a musician who said, "Okay, so we hired a lawyer and incorporated our band. We are an LLC. We have a Federal Tax ID # and have opened a bank account. Our operating agreement has been notarized and we are service and trademarking our name. What else should we be doing?"

"Uh… well, that's great, I guess. Sounds like you've got your ducks in a row. Why don't you send me some of your music and we'll go from there," I said.

"Oh, we haven't started the writing process yet. But as soon as we do, we'll send you some material," the band member responded.

Don't go to these extremes. Sure, it's good to discuss things in advance but don't get ahead of yourself. First make sure you've got the right musicians and songwriters to create brilliance. Afterwards, begin to talk about the business of your music. Without the brilliant music, none of the business matters.

ASCAP, BMI, or SESAC

A quick search on the Internet will lead you to any of these organizations. They are Performing Rights Organizations (PROs) that oversee the royalty collection for your songs. In the early stages of your career, when there are no real royalties to be collected, these PROs can be a valuable center of resources. They have endless opportunities and information available to their members.

Get involved. Go to music conferences and get to know people from these organizations. Choose one and sign up. You'll be amazed at the amount of information that can be found through PROs.

Which one is better than the other? Ask a dozen successful songwriters and you'll likely get an equal split as to their preference on which PRO is best. They're all good in their own unique way. Spend some time reading about and learning about each. Ask fellow musicians which PRO they belong to. Do your homework, but get signed up with one of them. Signing up for a PRO as a writer is free.

Merchandise is your friend

I can't tell you how many local band shows I've gone to where not a single piece of merchandise is available. Shocking.

But don't be fooled into thinking that just because you put your precious name on a T-shirt, people will buy it. Just like your music, it has to be great. In regard to T-shirts, I encourage bands to make T-shirts that people would want to buy even if they don't know or even like your band. Make your merchandise a uniquely creative extension of your music.

However, don't stop at T-shirts. Create other trinkets that would be desirable to your fans. In the 1980s it was patches, bandanas, and buttons. Today it's USB flash drives and organic tote bags.

Be careful not to over-extend your budget. Start slowly. Begin with a T-shirt. Make some money on that and turn that money into creating a second T-shirt. Talk to your fans. Find out what they want and give it to them, but don't over-extend your budget.

Remember, if you buy $500 worth of T-shirts and sell that batch for $1500, don't think you have $1000 disposable income. You're going to need to buy more shirts for $500. So don't go and spend your merchandise profits. Save some of those profits to re-invest in more merchandise.

A lot of times when I ask bands, "Why don't you have T-shirts?" they respond with, "We used to have them, but we sold out. When we get more money we'll buy more shirts."

You sold all your shirts for a profit, and have no money? Unfortunately, that's an extremely common theme in the local band merchandising world. Don't let it happen to you.

Q: *Jason from Greensboro, NC asks: What sources of income can an independent artist depend on now that they're basically expected to give away their music for free, and the money earned from playing small venues is barely enough to get from one gig to the next?*

A: There are a lot of creative ways to earn money outside of selling your music, although your live shows will likely be your bread and butter no matter how big you get. That's where you should plan on making the bulk of your money.

However, there's not a shortage of things you can sell merchandise-wise. Almost anything that you use in your daily life, from toothbrushes to shopping bags to cell phone cases, can be branded with your logo.

Focus on your merchandise and live performances. Chances are, if you can't make the money you need from those two sources, you may need to re-examine things a bit, perhaps write more songs or rehearse more. If you're not getting the gigs and not selling merchandise *at* those gigs, it's just not connecting with the audience like it should be.

The most commonly underutilized source of income for artists is merchandise.

Chapter 4:
All About Recording

5 common myths in recording

When making your first, second, or even third independently released recording, there are some common myths I'd like to dispel.

Myth #1: "People will care about my recording." Unfortunately just because you record music, doesn't mean people are going to automatically care. First, it has to be music that *moves* them. But how do you move them if they don't listen? Exactly. You're going to need a carefully constructed marketing plan that all comes together at once. Live shows, a video, social media, a website, and publicity. A carefully planned campaign around the release of your record. Don't make the mistake of thinking that once you're done recording people will care enough to seek you out and listen. They won't.

Myth #2: "The more songs I record for my CD, the greater chance I have of connecting with a listener." Wrong! For the same reason we always feel like there's nothing on television (when in reality we have 397 channels available to us at our lazy remote-control-holding fingertips), people will not dig through your entire CD to find the songs that connect with them. More often than not, they won't listen at all if there are too many options. Put your most brilliant songs on the CD and leave it at that. It's okay to have 2 songs on a CD if the songs are brilliant. If it's not a brilliant song, it should be left off. Remember: releasing too few songs on a CD is always better than releasing too many.

Myth #3: "A diverse recording is a positive thing, showing labels and industry professionals the many creative sides to my music." Wrong again. Like it or not, the industry likes to compartmentalize its music for ease of marketing. Not to mention, whether we are willing to admit it or not, we as music fans like to compartmentalize our music. One moment we may want to listen to a rock album. Later that night a jazz album, and on Sunday we're in the mood for reggae. But we don't want rock, jazz, and reggae all on the same album by the same artist. Rather than being viewed as diverse, the industry will view you as confused. Pick a style and stick to it, for this recording at least. And again, this is for your first few recordings. When you become Prince or The Beatles, experiment within your recordings. But as a newbie, you need to identify yourself, and your audience, with a genre they will understand.

Myth #4: "I will make money off my recordings." Unlikely. Your recordings should be your advertisement and/or your marketing tool for other streams of revenue like live performances, merchandising, and licensing. Do not make a recording with the anticipation of earning money on it. On that same note, don't go broke making a recording thinking that once it's released, you'll make your money back. It's very unlikely that will happen.

Myth #5: "Quality doesn't matter." Sorry, it does. People have limited time and they want to enjoy that time. When they choose to listen to music, they want a sound that is enjoyable. Sure, great songs can often cut through a crappy recording, but brilliant production won't make bad songs good. People like to listen to quality recordings. If they have to struggle to listen, they won't listen at all.

Make a (practical) recording

The method by which you record, the amount of money you spend, and the choice to have a producer largely depends on the stage of your career.

Is this your first recording? Don't spend tens of thousands of dollars to hire the best producer available. Have you released several recordings already, sold a lot of copies, and made your money back on them? If yes, then maybe it's time to pull out the big guns.

By the way, I use the word "album" to describe a recording of about ten or more songs. Some call it a record. Some call it an LP. But just so you know what I mean when I say "album," I mean a full-length recording usually consisting of about ten or more songs.

Let's talk about recording...

The first phonograph record was invented in 1877. By the 1950s and '60s, inexpensive portable record players were available to almost everyone. 45s soon became available, allowing the consumer to purchase single songs.

By the mid 1960s, eight-track players began to show up, and became very popular by the 1970s. The eight-track allowed the listener to select tracks, thus being able to skip around throughout the album. As the eight-track technology progressed, most players even had a fast-forward button on them, allowing you to skip through a song even more quickly.

The compact audio cassette tape became popular in the late '70s and remained one of only two primary formats (vinyl and cassette) through the early '90s. The cassette was amazing for music lovers. It was small and allowed users to become more mobile with their music. In the early '80s, Sony invented the Walkman, a portable cassette player with headphones that ran on batteries and allowed you to go anywhere with music. Cassette decks were standard in automobiles throughout the '80s. You could fast forward and rewind very easily, skipping around to hear the song or songs you wanted to hear and bypassing the ones you didn't.

By the early to mid '90s, Compact Discs, or CDs, had made their way into households around the world. We thought it couldn't get better for the music lover. It was the highest quality sound ever available. It was portable. You could take it anywhere as long as you had a player, and they soon became standard in automobiles.

For the first time in history, you could instantly skip to the song you wanted to hear. Ironically, CDs could hold more music than any previous format. As a result, record companies would release CDs with upwards of twenty or more songs. Music fans could now get high quality music, and a lot of it. They could take it anywhere they wanted, and they could skip the songs they didn't want to hear, giving them even more control.

Suddenly, it got even better with the introduction of the MPEG and subsequently the MP3. By the late '90s and early 2000s, music was being emailed around the world one song at a time. Napster launched in 1999, allowing music fans to download decent quality audio files for free. Chaos ensued in the recording industry. Lawsuits were flying between artists, record labels, and Internet companies offering free music. Even consumers were being sued for downloading free music.

Then, Apple came along in the early 2000s and launched iTunes. Now there was a legal and easy way for music fans to download music; either full albums or single songs.

Streaming music is now the most popular conduit for enjoying music. You don't even need to buy it. Just listen to it on demand on any number of available websites. Now, with smart phones, you can stream music anywhere.

Tomorrow it will be a different format. And ten years later, some new invention will further revolutionize the way we listen to music. And ten years after that, it will change even again.

But throughout history, time and again, music consumers have consistently proven they only want to listen to the songs they like. From eight-track to streaming radio, it has become increasingly easier for music fans to avoid songs they don't want to hear.

So what's the point of this little history lesson? Don't record music with the assumption that people will listen.

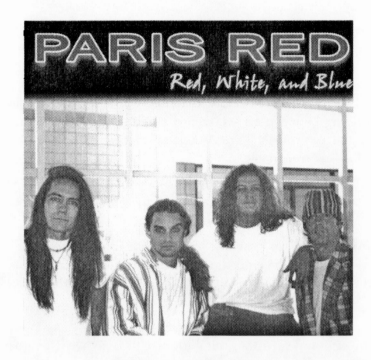

This was my first "real" recording.
It went certified Aluminum Foil, but it got us gas money from city to city.

Record your very best songs. Start by making basic, cheap demo recordings and slowly improve upon that process, making your recordings technically and musically better over time. Record frequently. Pay close attention to every detail -- most importantly, the song. Great songs can survive a mediocre recording, but great recordings won't make a mediocre song brilliant.

Q: *Terrence from Salt Lake City, UT asks: Does it matter if your demo is professionally recorded, or something you recorded on software you have at home?*

A: It depends on what stage you are in your career. In the very early stages, no, it does not matter. The purpose of your first few demos is either to get your songs heard, or to get your talent heard. As long as your demo is good enough to let the song or talent shine through, it's good enough.

But when you get to the point where you want your music to be available for public consumption and for sale, then yes, your recordings should sound professional.

Use your early demos to help determine which songs you should record. Ask friends and professionals which songs would be best to record, and then professionally record your two or three best songs.

I encourage artists to record dozens and dozens of home demos before spending the money on a professional recording, particularly if you are a songwriter. If the goal is to just get your vocal talents heard, you may want to venture into a professional studio a little sooner. But the art of songwriting takes time. It's unlikely the first 3 songs you write are refined enough to warrant spending the money on a professional recording.

Cousin Rick says: Set a date for your next recording. Mark it on your calendar, and then take the necessary steps toward keeping that goal.

Hiring a band

If you're a solo artist and interested in putting a full band behind your recording, the process of finding those musicians can be tough.

I suggest one of two solutions:

1. Find an existing local band that you like. You like their sound and instrument tones. Ideally, you like them as people, too, so you can work together on the project. Hire the entire band for the project. I recommend using a band that has been together for a while. Bands that have been together for a while are typically tight musically, they perform well together as a group, and that "kinship" will come through on the recording.

2. Depending on where you are in your career, you may be hiring a producer for your recording process. A good producer will work with you in shaping the overall project: the sound, possibly the arrangements of your songs, sometimes even the choice of studio (great producers usually have their preferred studios, but are able to work in any environment and can help find the location that's right for your sound and budget).

A good producer can also play a role in finding the right studio musicians to hire for your project. Studio musicians are a great option. It's like piecing together a cast for a movie. Based on your sound, a good producer will know which drummer, pianist, etc. in the area would be best to hire. Utilize the producer's knowledge of the local music community to help recruit the right people for the job.

Option 1 is the more cost-efficient method. Studio musicians are just that -- they are musicians who get hired to play in the studio. A good solid local band however may have never been asked to be the backing band on a recording project. Their day-to-day livelihood is their band. They make their money playing shows, selling music and merchandise, etc. So for them to go into the studio to play someone else's music might be a fun project for them. It's not to say you should expect to get them for free, but it will likely cost you less than piecing together the various studio musicians.

If option 1 sounds good to you, I encourage you to get to know and become friends with as many local bands as possible. Watch how they work together on stage. Are they people you'd like to work with? Furthermore, friends like helping friends -- perhaps if you're nice enough, you may get them at a very favorable rate.

How much should you expect to pay? That really varies depending on the level of the musician or band. I've seen studio musician rates vary from $300 to $3000 a song. Whereas, you may be able to get an entire local band for $300 a song or less.

Whichever route you take, do your homework. Don't be afraid to ask questions. If you're going down the road of the first option, ask five different bands that you like what they would consider a fair price to be the backing band on your recording. That will give you a good indication as to what is fair for your area. Bands in LA, New York, or Nashville would likely cost more than a band in Topeka, Kansas.

Sometimes you may even be able to offer a trade, but this gets a little risky in terms of the level of musicianship you might get. Perhaps you're a singer and you need a drummer, guitarist, and bass player for your recording. You could take out ads where you offer to sing on their recordings if they would play on yours. This is a little more time consuming and risky. You might get an A-level drummer, a B-level guitarist, and C-level bass player, thus bringing down the overall quality of your recording. But if you just don't have any money to pay musicians at all, possibly offering to trade your talent for theirs would be an option.

Hiring a producer

Finding a good producer for your recording project requires research. You first need to explore whether or not you need a producer. Do you need a producer or just a good studio and engineer?

The producer is the person overseeing the entire process and all elements involved in making the best recording possible. A great producer can make all the difference in the world for your recording. But you may not need a producer. A great producer can be helpful in the project, but isn't always necessary.

It's really up to you to decide how much help you need. You should be realistic in asking yourself that question. Could your songs use arrangement or instrumentation improvements? Are you unsure about where to record? Maybe you have 25 songs and need help narrowing it down to just a few. Are you hoping to have your songs on the radio? If so, are you confident you can get that radio sound without the help of a producer?

These are the types of questions you should ask yourself when deciding whether or not you need a producer. My advice is if you can afford a producer, hire one. They are almost always helpful.

So let's assume you've decided you need a producer. How do you find one? My best advice is to find out who produced recordings you like. You can do this by asking the artist who produced their record. It may be listed in the liner notes if you have the CD, or you can look on that artist's website in the album credits. Find recordings you like and find out who produced them. Be realistic though. If you're a local artist doing your first or second recording, reaching out to the producer of a mega-selling album may be out of your budget. Look local to start -- it will be your most cost-effective solution.

Look for locally produced recordings that you enjoy, and seek out those producers.

Then, meet with those producers. Give them your music and see what ideas they have. You should meet with a minimum of 3 producers before choosing the one that's right for you. A good local producer will be happy to meet with you to discuss your project prior to either of you committing.

Do your homework. Ask around to a *lot* of musicians that you respect. Whom do they recommend? You'll begin to find your answers pretty quickly.

Q: *Fran from Raleigh, NC asks: What is the ideal number of songs to have on a demo CD?*

A: Three songs. Other industry professionals may say differently, but for me, three songs give me the opportunity get a good snapshot of what the artist is all about. When I get a CD with 15 songs, I just don't have the time to listen to them, and sometimes, as a result, I don't listen at all. Three is a good number to start with.

Finding the right studio and engineer

First, and likely most important, is to listen to other music that was recorded at this studio or by this engineer. More often than not the studio will have some music posted on their website, but not always. Really search around and listen to as many recordings as you can that were done at this studio. It's not unreasonable to tell the studio or engineer that you'd like to listen to some of their previous work. Any real studio would be happy to oblige and will have confidence in their work.

Don't worry about what kind of equipment they have. Don't worry about how fancy their lounge may be, or how nice (or not nice) their building is.

A young band once said to me with enthusiasm after visiting a studio, "Dude. This place is awesome. They have an espresso machine in the lounge AND get this... they've got an Xbox gaming system too. And it's right across the street from a strip club."

Who cares? Do their recordings sound great? Does the engineer have a respectable work ethic, or will he show up hung over from his night out at the strip club?

Don't get dazzled by all the "cool stuff" when seeking out a studio or engineer.

Very simply, just listen to their work. If they consistently get great recordings out of a wide variety of genres, the likelihood is your recording will sound great as well.

Pricing is also a factor. Whether you're just starting out or you've sold a million records, I rarely see recordings come in under budget. It almost always costs more than you think it will cost. So, ask about pricing. Some studios charge an hourly rate. Some will work on a "per project" basis. Be sure to ask what is included in their pricing and if there are additional fees that you should be aware of. From there, plan your budget. How much can you really afford? And don't forget, after you record, you may want to have the recording mastered. That will cost extra. And if you are printing physical copies of the recording, plan for that in your budget too. What about art design? Will you need to pay for artwork and photography? Consider all those things in planning your overall budget.

Lastly, meet with the people you'll be working with. This is your music we're talking about, your heart and soul. So by all means, work with people you can tolerate being in a room with for hours on end. You've got to like the people you work with. If you're not "feeling it" when you meet with the engineer, then move on. Trust your instincts.

Q: *Dave from Long Island, NY asks: Is it marketable / desirable / profitable to be an album-oriented artist in today's music industry?*

A: Marketable? Yes. Desirable? Only for the die-hard fans. Profitable? Questionable.

The real answer to this question depends largely on what stage you are in your career. If you are a new artist, or an artist with a relatively small fan base, I don't recommend recording full albums at all. At that phase in your career, your goal is to capture the attention of new fans. Releasing 12 songs at once on an album makes that difficult. It's too much for them to absorb, so they just by-pass you altogether. If you're absolutely convinced that you have 12 brilliant songs, and you're a young artist, or an artist with a relatively small fan base, then you're better off releasing one song a month for the next year. You'll pick up more new fans that way.

However, if you're at the phase in your career where you do have a nice legion of die-hard fans, then yes, releasing full albums is certainly desirable for those fans. The die-hards want all they can get. It's difficult to give the die-hards too much music. Full albums can allow you the opportunity to strengthen your bond with your existing fan base. Even so, don't discount the need for a strong focus track. Create a video for this track and try to capture new fans that won't take the time to sift through your entire album.

Journalists and bloggers tend to pay more attention when you've taken the time to release a full-length album, though, so it could be argued that a full-album is more marketable than a single song or an EP. In this day-

and-age, there's definitely still an element of marketability to albums, particularly in the traditional press.

Profitable? Again, it sort of comes back to what stage you are in your career and how inexpensively you can record. Do the math ahead of time, and be realistic. Can you sell 1,000 CDs? If so, let's say that after manufacturing you make about $7.00 per CD. (These are just 'for example' numbers. You may make more or less depending on distribution, fulfillment, shipping, and manufacturing costs). 1,000 CDs at $7 each = $7,000. Do you have the ability to record a full album for less than $7,000, using this as an example?

That's all assuming you spend no money on marketing, advertising, publicity, a video, etc., which would, of course, be a mistake. Typically your recording budget should be about 25% to 50% of your gross sales projection depending on your financial goals. So in this example, if you felt you could sell $7,000 worth of CDs, I would suggest your recording budget should be between $1,750 and $3,500, so that you're able to spend some additional money on marketing, packaging, publicity, etc., and still make a small profit for yourself.

Simply do the math ahead of time. If you have never released a product, chances are your first should not be a full-length album. But if you have released product in the past, do budget projections based on past sales to determine if a full-length album can be profitable.

There's no doubt the days of full-length albums are dwindling, but as long as there is music -- brilliant music -- there will be fans that want more instead of less. Full albums are great and allow the artist to take us on a journey. Personally, I hope they never die, but they'll never be what they used to be.

Me, Jimmy Buffet, and Andy Martin
When you reach the status of Jimmy Buffett, full albums are marketable, desirable and profitable.

Chapter 5:
Booking, Venues, and Touring

One of my earliest mistakes

It was December 1989. I was in an '80s hair band that had been around a little less than a year. We had mostly played skating rinks and pool parties for our friends. To date we had no real club gigs to speak of... until now.

The big venue in my hometown of Raleigh was called The Switch. It's where all the touring bands played and it was our dream to get on the big stage there. The venue held about 800 people. I hung out there all the time as a young music fan.

My phone rang and it was the club owner for The Switch. He had an opening slot this upcoming Saturday for a band called White Heat. White Heat were regularly selling out that venue and eventually changed their name to Firehouse, got a big record deal, and went on to sell millions and millions of albums.

I remember calling my band mates saying, "We got our first club gig. And it's opening for White Heat!" Excitement was in the air. We practiced every night that week getting ready for the big gig.

When Saturday night rolled around, we were ready. We took the stage in full-on rock gear, leather jackets and all. As we looked out over the crowd of 800 people, we *knew* this was what we wanted to do with our lives. It was everything I imagined it would be. In 1989, at the only rock club in Raleigh, it was a tough crowd. You actually had to be pretty good to survive. We put on a great show totaling about thirty-five minutes. (When I say "great show," I mean -- we didn't get boo-ed or have things thrown at us. We were far from

My first club show. I had "made it."

brilliant, but we survived).

I think we played every original song we had that night, which was only about eight songs. We were on top of the world signing autographs after the show, selling tapes and T-shirts. In our mind, we had made it.

Now for the mistakes. Immediately following the show, the club owner took me back to his office to pay me the fifty dollars he had promised us. His office was no bigger than a closet, but I didn't care. It was the coolest thing I had ever seen.

He leaned back in his chair with a cigar between his fingers and said, "You boys are good."

He took a sip of what appeared to be whiskey and said to me, "Tell ya what, I've got an opening next Saturday night. You would headline the show. Find you a band to open for you and the slot is all yours. I can give you $100. Want it?"

Do we want it? I thought to myself, *Are you crazy? Of course we want it!* But I kept my cool and said, "Yeah, that sounds good. We'll take it."

But inside I was glowing and all smiles. We had made it. We got asked *back* to play the biggest venue in town, on a Saturday night no less. We were getting paid $100, and a crowd of 800 people just saw us perform. I was on top of the world!

We found an opening act and went back into rehearsals preparing for our big debut as a headliner. We had to learn some more cover songs to fill up the ninety minutes that would be required of us as a headliner, but we practiced hard and got them ready.

Saturday rolled around and the anticipation of another sold out show was on our minds. We were fully ready for another night rocking a packed house, signing autographs, and pretending to be rock stars.

Well, something went wrong. Something went horribly wrong! Only eight people showed up for our show that night. How could that be? We just played to 800 people the week before -- why didn't all 800 come back to see us again?

Oh, wait a minute. Maybe we needed to tell them we were playing again. Maybe we should have printed up some flyers and hung them around town. Maybe we should have asked for mailing information from people we met the week before. We could have mailed them a postcard and told them about the show.

The mistakes I made that week were numerous.

First of all, what the hell was I thinking booking a show one week later? Knowing now what I didn't know then, when the club owner said, "I have next Saturday night open," I should have realized that what he really meant was he had a band cancel and needed to fill it quickly. Since we were pretty good and happen to be sitting in the same room with him, he could fill it with us.

Had I played it smart I would have said, "We're actually booked next weekend, but let's look at something in six weeks." But I didn't. I made the classic mistake of thinking that the more I play, the more fans I will have.

Not to mention, when the club owner said, "You guys find

yourselves an opening act and you can headline," that should have translated to, "I'm really in no mood to find an opening act with only seven days notice. Why don't you do the work for me?" And we did. He was a smart guy, I'll give him that.

Why didn't those 800 people show up like before? Because, to get people out to a show you have got to *really* market it in every way possible. Not to mention you've got to musically move people to the core. We did neither. We were a decent band that thought we were better than we actually were and really didn't understand the need to market to people.

Playing to eight people that night was my lesson in the importance of marketing. I didn't make that mistake twice.

Additionally, I should have negotiated a percentage of the door after the one hundred dollars came through. Or some sort of bonus. *Remember*, I convinced myself that 800 people who just saw me open for White Heat were going to come back. Why I thought one hundred dollars would be just fine, I have no idea. The lesson I learned was to financially prepare for the best-case scenario. Negotiate your deals so that if it's a big win for the venue, it's a big win for you too.

Don't overplay the market. Don't expect people to come see you again just because they were forced to watch you as an opening act. Don't book a gig with only one week's notice when you're expected to fill the room. Always negotiate a deal that works for everyone if it's a big night.

I'll never forget that week of my life. I played my first big gig, and learned some extremely valuable lessons about how to build your audience in your hometown market.

Firehouse went on to sell millions of albums and win countless awards as artists and songwriters. Recently, I asked Bill Leverty (guitarist/songwriter for Firehouse/White Heat) a few questions about his early days:

<u>Me</u>: *In the late '80s almost any band generating any amount of local success moved to Los Angeles. You got a record deal and achieved worldwide success, yet you kept the southeast as your home throughout the process. Why did you not move to Los Angeles like so many other bands at the time?*

<u>Bill</u>: *We wanted to live where we were comfortable and able to be most productive. North Carolina and Virginia are great places to live. There was a good music scene here at the time too. LA was discussed, but dismissed as an unaffordable option, and we'd have to spend a lot of time trying to get established out there. We thought that if we could make good enough music, the labels would fly wherever we were playing to see us. We got about 4 showcases in NC for major labels (Atlantic, Geffen, MCA and A&M).*

<u>Me</u>: *During that time frame, White Heat (Firehouse) was known in the Southeast for regularly selling out the great music venues, like The Switch. From Virginia to Georgia, as an unsigned band, you guys would regularly sell-out rooms with a capacity of 500 or more. This was EXTREMELY rare during that time in music history in the Southeast. You obviously connected with people in a way other bands did not. To what do you attribute this connection with the fans that translated into sold-out shows?*

<u>Bill</u>: *I think it was because we got some local airplay, and back then, people listened to terrestrial radio!*

Cousin Rick says: What are your two biggest mistakes in the past 12 months? Just pointing them out to yourself will help you learn from them.

What matters in booking?

Let's take a moment to touch on some of the best methods to go about booking the right venues:

"Hello Mr. Venue Owner. I was calling to see if you've listened to our demo yet. We spent a lot of money at the best studio in town using the best producer in town. He really loved the songs. And our guitar player is a classically trained player from the University of Raleigh Music School. Our drummer has been playing since he was two years old. And I can promise you, we are as tight live as we are on the demo."

Whoop-di-do! Nobody cares, and certainly not Mr. Venue Owner of fifteen years in the business.

Try this approach on for size and see if it doesn't get you further:

"Hello Mr. Venue Owner. My band can put people in your venue. Lots of people. And more importantly, we will bring in drinkers. Our fans are over 21, they drink and we have a LOT of fans. We don't over-play the market. If we played your venue we wouldn't play another venue in town for 2 months and we'll spend the weeks leading up to the show marketing ONLY your show. I would expect realistically that we can put about 125 people in your room."

Hell, if you said that, you would probably have a date before getting off the phone. You could even wrap up that conversation by saying, "By the way, we're not even really that good. We're okay, but we're not great," and you'd still get the gig.

Venue owners don't care about the same things you do. They don't care how good your drummer is or where you recorded your demo. They want to know the room will be filled with drinkers. That's it.

So as you go into booking, keep that at the forefront of your mind.

Become a regular at the venue you want to play before you play the venue. Get to know the staff. They are the people who can help you market the show. Often they give the owner or booker tips on who they should be recruiting. Venues like to support musicians who support them. Support the venue where you want to play. Remember to speak to the owner or booker in their terms (bodies and drinkers) and, unless you're just absolutely horrible (and possibly even if you are), you'll almost certainly get the gig.

But once you *do* get the gig, you'd better follow through if you want to play there again. Continue to support the venue. Promote the show. Keep your promises of marketing and not overplaying the market. And most importantly, make sure you get people out to your show.

Build your market so that you can build others

As a young budding musician, a local booking agent that I respected once asked me how it was going with my band.

"Great!" I responded enthusiastically. "We have 12 shows this month alone, all right here in Raleigh."

He shook his head and said, "I hate to tell you, Dave, but 12 shows in one month in the same city actually isn't doing great."

A band's most common mistake, particularly in the band's early years, is overplaying the market. The theory being that the more we play out, the more fans we will have.

Unfortunately, that just isn't the case. In reality, the more you play your hometown market the more you dilute your fan base. Nobody can get *all* of their fans out to *all* of their shows *all* of the time. So, if you're playing in your hometown more than once a month, you're probably over-playing your market.

This doesn't necessarily apply to cover bands. The purpose of a cover band, more often than not, is to provide entertainment for a pre-existing audience. I'll touch on cover bands in their hometown market in a bit, but for the moment, let's focus on original acts interested in building a solid following locally.

Just because a gig comes your way doesn't mean you have to take it. Sometimes what you don't do is more important than what you do.

Be selective and pick a venue that is right for you. Don't think too highly of yourself either. Play a room that is the appropriate size for your current fan base.

Playing the biggest room in town isn't always the right move, and it's definitely not the right move if you can't come close to selling it out. You're actually better off playing a smaller room and selling it out than playing a larger room and it being only half-full.

Get to the point where you can sell out the smallest, but professional, live music venue in your area and move up from there.

My rule of thumb is to play your hometown market about every eight to twelve weeks. Make each show count. Make it an event. Care about the show and spend a lot of effort marketing it. You may want to consider printing some tickets and giving them away to friends and possible new fans in order to fill the room.

My suggestion to original artists from Raleigh, which is considered a mid-sized city, is to play about four times a year. In larger markets it's okay to play more, assuming you're playing different areas of the city. In smaller markets, play less.

Once you have sold out a venue in your hometown two or three times, it's time to expand your fan base to another market.

Do some research and find out what other band is also selling out a similar size venue in a neighboring town.

Find the band that's doing the same thing you are and contact them. It's quite simple from here. You say to them, "We are selling out to 150 people in our hometown but we've never played your town. Why don't you open for us on our next two shows in our town, and we'll come do the same for you in your town."

If you do this right, and really work that second market, pretty soon you'll have two markets you can sell out.

But the first step is getting your own market taken care of. Don't overplay the market. Play rooms appropriate for your fan base. Treat each show like an event, possibly even giving the show an event title, like "The First Annual _____ Fest."

If you're in a cover band, playing your hometown is more about strategic placement. Not only is it okay, it's expected for you to play as many shows as possible in your hometown. After all, if you're a cover band, you're partially (if not entirely) in it for the money. Sure, you like playing, but if you're playing someone else's music, you probably want to get paid, unless you're just purely a hobbyist, in which case, I thank you for buying this book despite it not being particularly useful to those only wanting to pursue music casually.

Let's assume as a cover band, you want to make money. The key to this is playing the right places. You may be a bar band wanting to play corporate gigs. Well, the bars are the perfect place to get those high-dollar wedding and corporate gigs. People will hear you at these bars. Play the right spots, and remember, dress for the part you want, not the one you have.

In every city, there are respectable bars for cover bands to play, and not so respectable bars. Usually, the respectable bars are gauged by the pay grade. The more a place pays cover bands, typically the more respected it is, at least in the cover band world.

Just like with the original bands, don't be afraid to say no to a gig opportunity. Pick the right venues and you'll soon find yourself moving up the ladder and gaining respect within the cover band community.

> *Cousin Rick says:* Plan a night to visit a venue you would like to play but haven't. It could even be an out-of-town venue. Plan a road trip. While you're there, introduce yourself to the staff members, preferably managers and owners.

Q: *Tobias from Houston, TX asks: What ratio of cover songs to originals should we play at live gigs?*

A: It depends on your goals. If you are primarily an original artist, I believe one or two cover songs thrown into a 60-minute set is appropriate. Choose songs that fit your style of course, but have fun with it. Everyone likes to hear the occasional familiar song. Throwing a cover song or two in your set can keep an audience interested.

I encourage even the biggest of nationally known acts to throw a cover song into their set. It's just something different that keeps the set fresh, while simultaneously paying tribute to an artist you respect.

If your goal, however, is to be a cover band, and a great working cover band, just reverse the formula. Maybe 1 original per set if you're a cover band, but even that's risky. As a cover band, people are typically there to dance, or listen to very familiar music. Your originals had better be damn good and fit within the context of the type of cover band you are. Generally speaking, I don't encourage cover bands to play any originals unless those originals are just downright brilliant and appropriate songs.

What is important to venues

The most important thing to remember in catching the attention of any venue is to communicate the things that matter to them, not you.

Make no mistake about it, most venues are in the alcohol business first, and the music business second. Not all, but most. Sure, they want great music, but they want great music because it sells alcohol, and they make the bulk of their profits on alcohol sales.

As always, there are exceptions. Some may make their money off of food. Some make their money off of coffee. But usually it's something other than the admission or ticket price that earns venues the bulk of their income.

So always keep that in the front of your mind when booking.

And with that in mind, a venue owner in Atlanta probably doesn't care that your guitar player went to Berklee College of Music. A venue owner in Nashville probably doesn't care that you opened for

Wilco once at a venue in Pittsburgh. They want to know what you can do for them, in *their* town, in *their* venue.

Can you bring out drinkers? Unless you have some sort of following in that city, the answer is probably "No."

So you need to use everything else you have. The first thing you need to do is relay the fact that you're not looking for a payday. Put money last on your list.

Do you have a team? Maybe you have an indie label that will help you with publicity. Or maybe you have a full-time social media person who will dedicate themselves to promoting this show.

Have you successfully grown other markets? How did you do this and explain to this venue how you plan to grow in their market.

Do you have *any* connections at all to this market? Even saying, "Three of my fraternity brothers from college moved there and they will help me promote the show" will help. Or, "My best friend lives in your city and he will really hit the streets promoting the show. Plus, he works at a place with 100 other people and he'll get a lot of those folks to come out."

Any connection at all that you have with the city in question, use it and make sure it's well known to the venue that you plan on using these resources heavily.

Be flexible and take whatever they give you. Go in there and prove yourself. Don't worry about the money. Play two or three times and prove that you can grow your fan base in that market. Do this, and I can almost guarantee the money will fall into place.

I own a small music venue in Raleigh, so I see firsthand every day how terribly most bands go about this. They usually tell us about how awesome their music is, or how well they do in their own hometown. Or sometimes they'll tell me about what a killer show they put on. But what I really want to know is: can they fill the room with people? Or at bare minimum, can they bring at least a few people to my venue?

Don't oversell yourself, either. That's worse. The bands that get the attention of my venue are honest. They may say, "We're new to Raleigh. We've never played the market. But we have about 10 close friends there and they'll come out. They'll also help us promote the show. We don't care about the money, or the night of the week that we play. We'd love to just get on a bill that you feel is appropriate and we promise we will do all we can to put 15 to 20 people there our first time in. And if it goes anything like it did in city A, B, and C, we should be filling your venue within six months to a year. And we're loyal. We'll stick with it as we grow if you'll give us the opportunity."

That sort of honesty would get almost any band a gig in my venue. I can see they'll work hard. They believe in themselves and they'll grow with me. As a result, I'm willing to give them a shot.

Remember, talk to the venue in a language they understand: bodies in the venue equals drinkers equals profits. Convince a venue you can put bodies in there and you'll get the gig. Once you do, you'd better make damn sure you follow through or you're going to be starting this process all over again with another venue, hoping they don't call the first one to find out how you did (they probably will).

A lot of venues rely on the headliner to choose their opening acts. Therefore, you should also research who is doing well in that venue and reach out to those bands.

Good luck. Breaking a new venue is difficult, but that's how you do it.

Q: *Josh from Denver, CO asks: For upcoming artists, is it a waste of time to do extensive touring far from their home base?*

A: Not completely. There are two primary reasons you should play out a lot as an upcoming artist: 1) To gain new fans, of course, and 2) To refine and tighten your live performance.

Make your out of town shows count. Don't travel eight hours to play a show unless you're pretty damn sure that you're going to be playing in front of some people. Not every show will be a winner, but do your homework and try to get on a bill that makes sense, one from which you can hopefully gain new fans.

Early on in your career, when you play an out of town gig to a small crowd, or worse -- to a crowd that consists solely of the bartender and soundman, make the night work for you and really focus on making your show better and tighter so that it's not a total waste of a trip.

Eventually, you need to start saying to yourself, "Is this worth it?" Is it worth traveling eight hours to play for ten people?

Here's a good gauge. If you travel eight hours and play to ten people, try it again in two months in the same town. Stay in touch with those ten people. Did those 10 people tell their friends so that you have 20 or 30 people attend your next show? If so, great! Try it again in two months. Did those 20 or 30 people tell their friends and now you've got 50 people in the audience? If that's the trend, then you're on the right track and yes, extensive touring far from your home base is working.

But if you play eight hours away in the same town on three different occasions, and your fan base isn't increasing even slightly, then something's wrong. It's just not connecting like it should. Go back home and write more songs and work on your show.

One of my favorite examples of this is Butch Walker. He played my hometown of Raleigh for the first time around 1996. Only about 15 people showed up, but those 15 people were absolutely blown away. I had a feeling something was going to explode with him. Sure enough, the next time he came to Raleigh those 15 people had passionately spread the word and 40 people showed up. By his third time playing Raleigh, he was selling out a 150 capacity venue. All of this happened in a six-month time frame. As I suspected, he went on to become one of the most respected artists, producers, and songwriters in the pop-rock world.

This is the sort of thing that needs to be happening with you. If it's working, people will tell people and your crowds will naturally increase. If your crowds aren't increasing, it doesn't necessarily mean you're bad, it just means something's not connecting. Get back home and figure it out.

Chapter 6:
What's Next?

The best advice I ever heard

Some of the best advice I ever received was from a songwriter named Terry Anderson. Terry has written several songs that reached the Billboard charts including the Dan Baird hit "I Love You Period."

Sadly, one of the best bands I ever played in only lasted about 6 months. The band was called The Hot Skillet Lickers and we released only one EP, "Lickin' It and Lovin' It." Terry Anderson was the drummer and primary songwriter for the group. Perhaps it's unfair to say it was one of the *best* bands, but The Hot Skillet Lickers did appear to achieve greater success than my other acts in relation to the time dedicated.

As all bands should be, but often are not, The Hot Skillet Lickers were put together purely for fun, with no expectations for success, only the expectation of writing songs that we liked.

The band formed in 1999 after I had already established a relatively stable Deep South Records. Terry Anderson also had stability in his main band The Olympic Ass-Kickin Team, and the other members of The Hot Skillet Lickers were at a place where a career as a musician wasn't exactly top priority. This band was just for fun, like my previous bands should have been, but weren't. Don't get me wrong, there had been elements of fun in all the bands, but I sometimes became stressed over the coveted goal of "making it big". Still, I've always managed to keep the idea of enjoying being in a band as a primary goal, but in the Skillet Lickers great songs and fun were the *only* goals.

We recorded our first song before we even had a name for the group. The song was called "Whoop Your Ass," an obvious tongue-in-cheek country song. I included the song as the closing track on the *Deep 3* compilation CD and assumed it would be remembered, or forgotten, as a mere comical moment known only to the few listeners who managed to make their way through to the final track of that disc.

Months after its release, I received a call from the organizers of a huge festival at the major amphitheater in Raleigh, Walnut Creek Amphitheater. They wanted The Hot Skillet Lickers to perform. While I was flattered, my first thought was, *"We're not even a band. We only have one song!"*

I went back to the other guys, asked if they'd like to try to do a show, and we hastily put together 45 minutes worth of material in a few short weeks. We agreed to do this one-time show just for fun, playing a set of songs written primarily by Terry. Song titles such as "I Wish I Was Your Thong" and "Cornbread" made it difficult for us to take ourselves too seriously, which would turn out to be our most valuable asset.

After our performance I casually walked around to the different merchandise stations scattered throughout the amphitheater pavilion and asked the attendants, *"Who's selling the most merchandise today?"* This was common for me to do at all festivals. It gave me a good indication as to who I should be keeping an eye on as a budding young record executive. Naturally the bands selling the most merchandise were the bands the fans most enjoyed. Surprisingly, at all 3 of the merchandise stations I received a quick and definitive answer:

"Well, that's hard to say. But if we *had* merchandise from The Hot Skillet Lickers, *that* would be our biggest seller. Everyone's been requesting that band the most." We weren't even a real band, so we certainly didn't have merchandise available.

Keep in mind, these merchandise attendants had no idea I was *in* the band. Merchandise stations in amphitheaters are located in areas where the workers can't even see the stage. They're positioned typically by the front gate or out in the breezeway or food court, so the workers who were telling me about lost sales for The Hot Skillet Lickers merchandise just assumed I was a curious customer.

Partially thrilled that my band was the hot item on the bill, I was mostly bewildered. How could I have spent the better part of my life focusing on a successful career as a musician, and *this* be the band that somehow connects with the public? This was a band that started as, and remained, a quickly thrown together joke with no intentions of even playing a show, much less a successful show.

How could I have studied books, and networked religiously at music conferences during my tenure in other acts only to have it not connect like this band appeared to be connecting? I had carefully crafted career paths for my previous bands only to fall short, yet here was a band that was not even really a band and it was somehow reaching people.

So we did what musicians do when faced with a moment of success -- we went and recorded some more songs with intentions of doing a few more shows, while agreeing this would remain a side project to our "real" lives.

Next thing we knew, we found ourselves getting regular airplay on one of the most popular nationally syndicated morning radio shows. We found ourselves getting offered coveted opening slots for national touring acts. We received nationwide attention from new fans yet we had only played a couple of shows as a band.

As the success started to trickle in, we started to wonder if we should try to get serious about this. Perhaps we should think about making it a priority and really focus for a while. After all, we had all been in countless bands in the past that took years to achieve even a fraction of the success this band was starting to see.

Then one night, as we were about to take the stage to a sold out crowd of 400+ people in our hometown of Raleigh, Terry stopped us just before we walked on and said with the most serious of looks on his face (yet still with a hint of a smile), "*Hey. If I catch anyone giving a shit out there on stage, you're gonna get an ass whoopin'.*" That night, when I least expected it, I got some of the best advice I had ever heard.

I realized this band was successful *because* we only had intentions of having fun, not despite that fact. The Hot Skillet Lickers were becoming noticed because we didn't *care* about becoming noticed. This is not to say that the act of not caring alone will bring you recognition. It's only to show by example that we were having fun creating great music, because creating great music *was* the goal, it *was* the fun, not a means to the goal.

While Terry's advice was simple and light-hearted in nature, it has a resounding implication that all bands should adhere to: Always remember that the music, and the enjoyment of the music, *is* the goal. Once you start to care *too* much about things that really aren't that important -- once you start "giving a shit," as he so eloquently put it, you will begin to care about the wrong things if you're not careful. You begin to focus on what the music might bring you -- fame and fortune -- instead of remembering that the music *is* the goal.

I'll never know what would have happened with that band had we continued along a path of not giving a shit. We quietly went our separate ways after only 8 shows. There was no ceremonious break-up. We simply all had our own obligations -- me with Deep South, the others with their families and careers.

Care about the music, and the joy it can bring you, and you'll be surprised how many new doors will open because of it.

> *Cousin Rick says:* Next time you're about to take the stage with your band mates, remind them in your own words that the only thing they can do wrong during the show is to *not* have fun. The only thing that could make the evening sour would be the moment somebody on stage starts "giving a shit."

What you *don't* do is as important as what you *do*

Early on in my professional relationship with Bruce Hornsby, an opportunity came across my desk for him to appear on a national television show. I was excited. It seemed like a great opportunity for him to be seen by millions who would hopefully discover his new record.

Washington, DC - October 2000
L to R: Andy Martin *(Deep South)*
Bruce Hornsby
Dave Rose *(Deep South)*

This picture was taken when Bruce performed
for President Clinton at the President's Cup Gala.

Every artist I have ever managed has taught me something. Most have taught me a *lot* and one who is very high on that list is Bruce Hornsby.

Out of respect for the show, I won't mention its name. As I was on the phone with Bruce running through a list of topics for the day, we discussed this television appearance. He quickly told me he wanted to pass.

"What?" I responded surprised, thinking maybe I didn't explain the opportunity properly. "Really? This is a national TV show with big ratings right now. Are you sure you want to pass?"

And he said something to me that has always stuck and I will never forget.

He said confidently, "The short-term benefits are debatable and uncertain at best, but the long-term negatives could potentially run much deeper."

I was so blown away by that insight I didn't even care that he was turning down a TV show. I instantly wrote that statement down on a piece of paper. I knew it would be something I'd want to remember for the rest of my career. If memory serves me correctly, I even asked him to repeat it to make sure I got it word for word.

From that day on I had an even higher level of respect for Bruce and it helped me tremendously in having a better understanding of him and his career. It would also help me on countless other occasions in the future.

Just as playing more notes in a song doesn't necessarily make the song better, doing more "stuff" in the public eye doesn't necessarily make your career more stable. Sometimes what you don't do is more important than what you do.

Bruce Hornsby knows exactly who he is. He's confident in himself and his music. He knows that sometimes the wrong move can have more negative than positive effects. This seems like common sense. It's certainly something I should have known prior to entering the business world with a legend like Bruce Hornsby, but it took him saying it so eloquently to really make it sink in with me.

He was right. Just because someone says, "Would you like to play this gig?" or, "Would you like to do this interview?" doesn't mean you should do it. Look at the long-term effects of everything you do. Sometimes saying, "Thanks, but no thanks," can be the best thing you can do for your career.

BRUCE HORNSBY

Dave,

You're one of the best guys
I worked with over these twenty years —
Thanks for that. Hope you're well,

Hope to see you sometime.

Love,

Bruce

Cousin Rick says: Name an event or opportunity in the past six months that you said "yes" to where you should have said "no."

Q: *Mike from Poughkeepsie, NY asks: How can you identify a dishonest person in this business?*

A: I once had a bar owner tell me, "Everyone in the bar business steals. The trick is to find the ones who steal the least."

Not everyone in the music business is dishonest. A lot are, but not all. Find the ones who are the least dishonest. Identifying a dishonest person in the music business is just like identifying a dishonest person in any business. A lot of it is gut instinct. If it smells funny, don't eat it.

Do your homework. Find people who have worked with the person or company in question. Ask them their opinions, and do this a lot. I always recommend that anyone considering going in to business with me talk to others I've been in business with in the past. If the person in question has nothing to hide, they will welcome the opportunity to be checked up on.

Notice "The Moments"

Study the careers of great musicians and you will discover the moments that changed their lives. Almost anyone who shines in their respective field, whether they be business people, entrepreneurs, actors, or inventors can tell you about *their* life changing moments. Notice *your* moments and why they are so life changing. Study the people or events behind these moments.

For me, one of those moments was October 26, 2003.

I was flying from Raleigh to Las Vegas to oversee part of the Stryper reunion tour, their first tour since 1991. Wanting and needing to be as hands on as possible with the regrouping of an iconic band, I went to as many shows on that tour as time would permit.

On my flight there I finished reading Gene Simmons's book "Sex, Money, and Kiss". I'd call that a life changing moment, not necessarily because I subscribe to all of his philosophies (although I do admire him greatly as a businessman), but more so because the book is a compelling read on success in the music business. Those who have followed Gene's career know that he's quick to sing his own praises, so to speak. He's quick to point out his greatness, and the book is no different. However, in his book he also discusses failures, both professionally and personally. He discusses the marriage of art and commerce in great detail, and how to make smart decisions in life whether you are a musician or not. This book would have been more appropriately titled "The Gospel According To Gene." It's chock full of his opinions on how to be successful and many of them were incredibly insightful to me.

As I was exiting the plane I even made note of this life-changing moment, saying to my business partner, Andy, "Wow. I'll never forget this day. October 26, 2003. The day I finished Gene Simmons's book."

In the afternoon we went about business as usual with Stryper sound-checks and band meetings.

The show sold out that night. After congratulating the band and some post-show small talk, Andy and I decided to head out. The concert was over relatively early, around 10:30pm or so.

On our way back to the hotel we wanted to stop off somewhere for a drink and to re-cap the evening. We found a quiet empty bar with only about 5 or 6 people inside. I like quiet bars after a concert. After ordering a round of beers, Andy and I were standing near the bar making small talk when his eyes lit up. I had never seen such a surprised look on Andy's face and he quickly, but quietly, said, *"Don't look now, but Gene Simmons is standing right behind you."* I could only assume this was a joke, since it was just hours earlier when I told Andy that reading Gene's book was a life changing moment for me.

Sure enough, I indiscreetly glanced over my shoulder and Gene Simmons was standing not more than an arms length away.

October 26, 2003 just went from life changing to surreal. I didn't know it at the time, but Gene was in town with Kiss playing a show with Aerosmith. And of the 9,723 bars in Vegas, he just happened to be in the same empty bar at the same time as me.

Imagine this. Think about the best book you've read in your entire life, and think about the day you finished reading this book. Now imagine being in a city where the author does not live, and imagine running in to that author in a small bar... all by chance. What are the odds?

"It's meant to be," I said quietly to Andy. "I've *got* to meet him."

From reading Gene's book I knew that he was not a drinker, so two sips in on my first beer, I sat it on the bar, pushed it away from me, and turned around to introduce myself. I don't get star struck, and I wasn't really star struck then, but I did want to carefully plan my introduction. *"What should I say?"* I debated.

Like ripping off a Band-Aid, sometimes it's best to not over-think things, so I just jumped right in before I lost the moment.

"Hi. I'm Dave Rose. I own a management company called Deep South. We manage Stryper who happen to be playing in town and I just wanted to introduce myself," I said nervously. *Was that too forward? I* thought. *Too much information in the first few sentences? What if he's at this small bar because he doesn't want to be seen or talk to people?*

"Nice to meet you, Dave," he said extending his hand for a handshake. "That's great, how long have you been managing them?" the fire-breathing God of Thunder asked quietly, and seemed to be genuinely interested.

We continued our conversation for another 30 minutes or so. Word of his presence had started to spread and the bar began to fill up. Within the hour, beautiful ladies and fans were all around us. It was still relatively subdued -- it wasn't a party bar, but instead more of a lounge. Each time someone would come to introduce themselves to Gene, I would politely offer to bow out of the circle, saying to him, "Well, I'll let you do your thing. It was nice meeting you."

"No. No. No. Stay," he would say. Then he would say to whoever was wanting to meet him, "Hi Jim / Nancy / Ms. August Centerfold... Have you met my friend, Dave?" and he would introduce them to me. *Have you met my friend, Dave?* Really? Less than 5 hours ago I was in the middle seat on a Southwest airplane eating peanuts and drinking diet coke reading (more like studying) his book. *Have you met my friend, Dave?*

True to his words in the book, Gene was not drinking that night. When I read that Gene never drank, I didn't believe it. No way could that be true -- but it was. We stayed and talked and met his fans for hours -- each time, he made sure I was introduced.

Gene is very secure in himself. Many would call him pompous. At one point in the evening Ms. August Centerfold (Disclaimer: I don't recall that August was the actual month -- I just remember meeting a monthly centerfold model) introduced herself to Gene and the first words out of his mouth were not, "Nice to meet you," instead they were, "Do you think my friend, Dave here, is attractive?"

Confused, she hesitantly responded, "Uh... Yeah... Sure, I guess." I'll take that. I'm okay with "Uh, yeah, sure. I guess" from Ms. Whatever-her-month-is.

"Give him a kiss," Gene said directly. Again, hesitant and somewhat confused, she looked at me and shrugged her shoulders and said, "I'll play along. You okay with that?" I was equally as puzzled and unsure, but always up for a good game of "Kiss the strange Centerfold model," we proceeded in an awkward peck on the lips with as much passion as kissing your aunt Trudy.

She chatted for a brief while and then went on about mingling.

Gene, unlike anyone I had ever met, was acutely aware of his celebrity status and the power it could carry, and he was not ashamed to notice the effect a celebrity could have on people, nor was he ashamed of exploiting it.

In his book he talked about how he might be the oldest, ugliest guy in the room, but if he wanted to, he could steal your wife away. I believe it.

Hours turned into more hours as Gene and I continued to chat, and meet his fans. Regularly I would gauge my welcome by offering to remove myself from what had become somewhat of a fan-frenzy. He continued to encourage me to stay with him.

Eventually, closing time came. Yes, apparently some bars do close in Vegas. Gene and I exchanged genuinely friendly parting words. He even asked me to walk outside with him so we could say our good-byes in less of a crowded area. I obliged. We shook hands along with the standard pleasantries of "Let's stay in touch" and "Nice to meet you."

We didn't stay in touch. But that's okay by me. October 26, 2003 changed my life. I read a book from one of the finest branding and marketing minds in the music business, and in the same day I got to spend 5 or 6 hours being known to strangers as "Gene's friend, Dave."

When your moment arrives, notice it. When you have an opportunity to spend time with someone who can teach you something, don't blow it. Take a chance. Talk to the person. Even if you learn something small, it's all worth it. Notice your moments. Pay attention to your opportunities. You never know when that moment may come but when it does, seize it.

> *Cousin Rick says:* Write down your 3 most life changing moments. The sheer act of writing them down will help you analyze why they were monumental and will help you study how they can relate to your career.

Everyone is smarter than you

Everyone is smarter than you about *something*. Seriously, understand this basic concept as it applies to the music business and you'll be amazed at what you can learn.

Think of the biggest idiot you know. Someone that you feel is just plain stupid. Even *that* person knows something that you don't. And because you spend your energy focused on how dumb they are, you'll never learn that one nugget of information they posses that you don't that could prove beneficial to you one day.

There's an unfortunate sense of hierarchy in the local band world. Bands that play bigger venues, have more fans, and sell more merchandise certainly must be better, and smarter, than the opening acts performing before them on the bill, right? As a musician, don't buy into this hierarchy. Learn something from every musician you meet, because they ALL know something that you don't.

Maybe they know the best website to buy cheap guitar strings. Or maybe they know how to fix a broken radiator hose in a band van. Or maybe you can learn a small piece of fashion advice by noticing a cool pair of shoes or something they are wearing. Or maybe they know of a place to get flyers printed cheaply. Or maybe they have a friend at a booking agency.

Everyone is smarter than you about *something*. Learn from everyone you meet in the music business. Because they all, even those just starting out, know something that you don't. If you spend all of your mental efforts concerned with yourself, you'll never open up enough to learn from those around you.

When you find those few special people that you feel really have it together -- those people you look up to -- spend as much time with them as they will allow. Make these people your mentors. Even the biggest idiot can teach you something, but a great mentor can really change your life.

I'm not really sure why, but it wasn't until recently that I understood the importance of having mentors, probably because I incorrectly felt there needed to be some sort of formalization of the mentor status. It's silly, but I felt I needed to actually say to a person, "Will you be my mentor?" almost like in the 6th grade when I asked Missy Fulmer if she would "go with me." Truth be told, most of the mentors I've had in my life probably don't even know I considered them as such.

Learn something from everyone, but find a few who have achieved greatness and learn a lot from those people.

This would probably be an appropriate place in the book to thank some of my mentors -- people who have taught me a lot over the years.

Joe Rose. Thank you for teaching me how to be a man. Not necessarily a man that can wrestle a grizzly bear or rebuild a carburetor in a '66 Mustang with nothing more than a Swiss army knife; although as a kid, I believed you could do both those things at the same time, and more. But thank you for teaching me to be a man that's not afraid to love, to be honest, to work hard, to treat people with respect, and (when necessary) a man who is not afraid to stand up for his players and yell at the umpire when he's made a bad call.

Ruth Rose. Thank you for loving me unconditionally, especially when I must have looked like an idiot in some of those clothes I used to wear. I don't recall you ever telling me to cut my hair or grow up, although both would have been justified requests. Thank you for being so smart. You're smarter than any scholar I know, yet you chose a much more difficult career path -- being a mom and raising your two kids. Thanks for that.

The following people have taught me a lot about life and/or the business of music. I am grateful to them in ways they may never know (in no particular order): Phil Zachary. Michael Sweet. Bruce Hornsby. Bill Payne. Allison Moorer. Butch Walker. Vienna Teng. John Wozniak. Jay Williams. Greg Gallo. Matt Thomas. Josh McSwain. Scott Thomas. Barry Knox. Amy Cox. Andy Martin. Kevin Frazier. Jay Nachlis. Mike Hartel. Doug Grissom. Bob Jamieson. David Bendeth. Bill Leverty. Harry Poloner. Charles Meeker. Rhonda Beatty. Virginia Parker. Mark Paris. Tim Gaines. Robert Kearns. Philip Isley. Nancy McFarlane. Matt Smith. Bev Paul.

Vienna: the artist, not the city

Every musician reading this should set aside some time to study the career of Vienna Teng. Research her on the Internet. She is a singer, a songwriter, and a pianist.

Her story is absolutely amazing, and should be taught to anyone hoping to have a career in music. Vienna was a student in the Bay Area at Stanford University studying computer science. About mid-way through her tenure, she decided she wanted to become a professional musician, but she knew this would require discipline and money.

So she put a plan in place and stuck to it. Her plan included working hard and finishing school, in hopes of landing a well-paying job upon graduation. Follow along here: The knee-jerk reaction most artists have when choosing music as their career is to give up everything. If they don't give up on it physically, they most often at least give up on it mentally. Most musicians have their "I'm going to be a musician" moment and instantly quit school (or a job) and focus all their efforts on music. Not Vienna. She instead focused *more* on school, and *more* on graduating high in her class. Why would she do such a crazy thing, knowing she wanted a career in music?

Stanford had recording studios that students could use for free while enrolled. Slowly and quietly, while still putting her studies first, she recorded an album at the school's studio. She finished her final two years of college, and graduated very high in her class. Upon graduating, she was offered a nice paying job in the field of computer science. She took it, still knowing music would be her career.

Again, this goes completely against what most musicians would think is the right move. Most, upon finally graduating would say, "Whew. I'm done. Finally. *Now* I can concentrate on music." They would likely get a job at some local restaurant or bar, offering them the freedom to pursue music. Not Vienna. She got her high-paying job and lived cheaply. She rented an apartment located nearby, so she wouldn't need a car. She had several roommates to keep her living costs down. And while many from her graduating class were out buying new cars and houses with the money they were earning, she decided to save for her career in music.

While working her day job, Vienna released her first album, *Waking Hour*. She played gigs in her spare time and promoted that record the best she could. She had a two-year plan to work and save as much as possible before she would leave corporate America to pursue a career in music.

I went to a Christmas Party in 2002 for Redeye Distribution. Making small talk with the owner of Redeye over some eggnog, I asked, "Who's doing well for you these days? Who's selling records?"

He thought for a while and said, "Well, there is this girl from San Francisco that's doing pretty well. It's mostly online sales, but in the past month she's really started moving some product. I'm not completely sure what her whole story is, but her name is Vienna Teng."

I got a copy of the album and it all made sense to me. No wonder she was starting to do well. The songs were, and still are, brilliant.

144

Right after Christmas I got on a plane headed to San Francisco to hear her perform.

She was playing at a Borders bookstore on a Saturday afternoon in the city. There were probably about 30 of us in the audience. The performance was incredible. She arrived, set up her own keyboard, and throughout the show spoke to the audience as if we were all friends. Then, at the end of the show, she very quietly said, "If anyone would like a copy of my album, I'll be sitting over here selling them after this song."

The *entire* audience of 30 people got in line to purchase the album after her performance. Seriously, not a single person walked out. I had never before seen a performance where 100% of the audience liked the music *so* much that they bought the album. Now keep in mind, these weren't her friends. Her friends already owned the album, as it had been out for a while. No, these were strangers who just happened to be in Borders that day and stumbled across this talented young lady playing some songs. Or perhaps they had heard about her from friends and wanted to come hear her firsthand to see what all the hubbub was about.

Total strangers heard her perform once, and bought her album.

Just prior to that performance at Borders, she had sent a copy of her album to National Public Radio, and despite not having all the "big label" backing, someone took a listen and fell in love with it. David Letterman just happened to be driving home from work one day, listening to the radio, and heard this relatively unknown artist. He called his producer from his car and said something along the lines of, "I don't know who this girl is, but I want her on the show."

Within about 10 days of seeing her perform at Borders, I watched Vienna Teng become one of the very few 'local' artists to perform on The Late Show with David Letterman.

The very next day after performing on The Late Show she went Top Ten on Amazon.com -- they were immediately backlogged with orders.

It wasn't long until her two-year plan of working a day job started coming to an end; on her two-year anniversary, she quit. She had saved an incredible amount of money, enough to pay to record her second album all on her own *and* to live for a couple of years while she worked on music and built a career. She had no major label money and no financial support from friends or parents. There were no crowd-funding platforms like Kickstarter back then. She worked for two years saving money, knowing that those two years fresh out of college would be her best opportunity to make the most money possible to support herself while she got her music career off the ground.

Once she was free to become a professional musician, we started shopping her around to record labels.*

In the interest of keeping this story as short as possible, I have not mentioned Virt Records and do not want to take any credit away from them by failing to discuss their important role. This one-man-label from Seattle believed in Vienna from the beginning and released her first two albums. They distributed those albums through Redeye, which is how I heard about her at the Christmas party. Oddly enough, the founder of Virt works for Amazon now.

Rounder Records became interested almost immediately. Vienna booked some gigs around the Boston area, where Rounder is located, and invited the label out to a show. My co-worker (and still to this day, Vienna Teng's manager), Amy Cox, and I flew to Boston for the gig. It was an unorthodox show at Harvard University in a ballroom. I say "unorthodox" because it wasn't really a "concert" type event. There was a dinner and awards were being presented. Vienna's performance was just *part* of that evening.

Amy and I sat with the executives from Rounder Records during the show. It was brilliant, and the Rounder folks seemed to think so as well. Vienna played to about 125 people that night. As the show came to a close, she mentioned to the audience that she would be at a table beside the stage selling her CD.

The show was almost over as Vienna was ringing out her last notes on the piano and the Rounder executives turned to Amy and me, saying something to the nature of, "That was a great show. We really liked it. Let's talk more."

I remember saying, "Wait. Don't leave yet. You haven't seen the most amazing part."

"What? Does she do an encore?" a label executive asked.

"Just wait and watch," I said.

Vienna humbly stood up from her piano stool and walked over to her merchandise table and people immediately flocked over to purchase the CD. I don't mean just a few people... it was a line of over 100 people forming along the side of the room (about 80% of the audience).

Great marketing doesn't create that kind of reaction in music fans. Publicity or social media won't cause 80% of a room to purchase a CD immediately following a performance. No, none of those "how-to" things we learn about the music business can cause 100 people to form a line to buy a CD from an artist they just heard. Only one thing can do that: undeniably brilliant music that has reached into the very soul of each individual who is listening.

Vienna Teng signed a record deal with Rounder within the month.

My cousin Rick told me about BOSTON because the music moved his soul. When I saw Vienna in Borders playing to 30 people, all 30 people were moved so intensely that they *had* to purchase the CD. The selling point to Rounder Records was witnessing first-hand the way Vienna Teng's music touches people. In a room of 125 people, 100 of them lined up to purchase the CD. It wouldn't surprise me if the other 25 already had the CD. This has happened *all* the time throughout Vienna's career. Besides that performance on Letterman, she has never had a huge moment in the spotlight as far as the traditional music business is concerned.

Fortunately, she doesn't need it because her fans are her advertising billboard. Once you hear Vienna Teng, you *have* to tell someone else about her. She's just that good.

Not long ago she got the opening slot for Shawn Colvin, playing amphitheaters to thousands of people. On the first night of the tour, before her last song, she said, "I'll be out in the pavilion selling my CD if you'd like one."

Boston, MA - April 2005
L to R: Dave Rose (Deep South)
Vienna Teng
Amy Cox (Deep South)

The night Rounder Records came to hear Vienna Teng.

Shawn Colvin had to delay her set 45 minutes that night because such a HUGE amount of people went out to the pavilion to buy Vienna Teng CDs. For the remainder of that tour, and out of incredible respect for Shawn Colvin, Vienna waited until Shawn was done playing before going to the pavilion to sell her albums, even going so far as to let the audience know she would be waiting until after Shawn's performance to start selling her CD.

This is the effect brilliant music has on people.

Don't worry about understanding a publishing deal before you've made undeniably brilliant music. Don't worry about getting email addresses for every industry executive in the world. Don't worry about entertainment attorneys, managers, and booking agents - not until you've made music that can move people like Vienna Teng's music moves people. Make brilliant music first. Music that moves people to go to endless extremes to get it, and to tell people about it -- like my cousin Rick did. And like Vienna Teng fans do every day.

Managers, contracts, royalty points, publishing deals: none of that matters! Not yet. Don't worry about that stuff until you are moving people to the very core of their soul.

Vienna Teng didn't achieve success because she knew the right person to contact at that radio station in New York. In fact, she didn't know anyone at that radio station. She just blindly sent them the album.

And that album touched them.

She didn't get on Letterman because she knew the right people or because she had the secret phone number for the producer. She got on David Letterman's show because after one listen, the music moved him.

She didn't get a record deal with Rounder because she had all the right contacts or great relationships there. She got a record deal because her music moved them, or more importantly, it moved the people who were in the audience when Rounder was watching.

Make music that moves people, and things will take care of themselves.

Fast-forward, and Vienna Teng continues to sell out theaters and rooms worldwide. She is not a household name, but she doesn't need to be. She has done what she set out to do. She has a great career in music, all because she had the discipline to stay the course, and during that course, she focused on making brilliant music. Music so amazing that your cousin Rick would just *have* to tell you about it at the next family reunion.

Dave:

Just wanted to thank you for taking on me & my music so early on, and for always having the right approach to this career. I've really valued your help & ideas... please keep 'em coming!

Let's enjoy the ride —

Vienna

Cousin Rick says: Listen to two Vienna Teng songs or watch two of her videos.

Q: *Kendra from Hollywood, CA asks: Why won't mainstream radio even consider playing your song if you're not a heavy hitter?*

A: Mainstream radio is just that, music for the mainstream. Most radio is music for the masses. It's a place for people to go to be comfortable listening to something familiar. Don't worry about mainstream radio. Worry about getting your songs heard by the masses on the Internet and at your live shows.

A member of the band Little Feat once told me, "The best thing that ever happened to us was not having a huge radio hit." That's questionable to some, because they do have some pretty notable radio hits, but they were never huge on the radio. Yet, they have continued to make a great living in music for over 30 years.

Don't live or die by radio; you shouldn't be concerned with whether or not they play your music. What you should be concerned with is this: Are the attendance numbers at your shows increasing? Are your fans really, really, passionate about your music? Are they telling their friends about you in huge numbers? All the radio spins in the world won't sustain a 30-year career without fans that genuinely care about you.

It's *your* music. Make it personal.

I've always appreciated the songwriting of Allison Moorer. Allison is wife to Steve Earle and sister of Shelby Lynne. She received an Academy Award nomination for her song "A Soft Place to Fall," which was in Robert Redford's *The Horse Whisperer*. She did the single version of Kid Rock's song "Picture" (most people know the female voice on that song as Sheryl Crow, but if you purchased the single version, it came with Allison Moorer's voice). She's had five singles on the Billboard charts.

Yet none of these accomplishments define Allison Moorer. Her music is far more than a Billboard hit and she is much more than an Academy Award nominee. I managed Allison for a few years, and I learned a lot from her during that time.

Songwriting is personal -- *very* personal. That is something I was never able to fully grasp until working with Allison. Prior to Allison, most of the artists I had worked with were "hit-makers" or at bare minimum they were aspiring hit-makers. Previously, I primarily worked with artists who either had some radio hits, or who were constantly trying to have a radio hit. But that's okay -- that was their goal -- that was their definition of success.

Allison didn't care about hits. But not in a "I-don't-have-any-hits-so-I'm-going-to-pretend-I-don't-care-about-hits," kind of way. She actually did have hits, and she had all the skills to have become a hit-making factory if she had wanted. But it likely would have meant some musical sacrifices.

Make no mistake about it folks, hits are a formula. There are actually websites that study current hits in an analytical fashion. They show you all the statistics of current hit songs: the average length of time before reaching the first chorus, the primary instruments, the average length intro, outro, etc. Practice that formula long enough and you too can likely have a hit.

But, it may come at a price.

Remember earlier in the book when I talked about defining success? You've got to clearly define exactly what it is you want in order to obtain it. You can't be successful if you haven't defined your idea of success.

Allison Moorer's idea of success was not about how many hit songs she could chart. It was about writing songs that were deeply personal and meant something to her.

When listening to Allison's songs, it was as if I could hear her reaching into the depths of her soul and somehow miraculously transferring those emotions onto a recorded medium. To her, that was success. If she could take her thoughts, feelings, and the very core of her being and translate that into a song, it was a successful song.

This isn't to say that she would turn her nose up at commercial success, but she wasn't willing to obtain it at a price of sacrificing *her* idea of success, which was doing songs her way, musically *and* lyrically.

I made a big mistake early on with Allison. I incorrectly assumed that her idea of success was similar to that of other artists I had managed. Commercial success at any price. Hit songs at any price. Mainstream acceptance at any price.

Nope, not Allison.

Allison did (and still does) things her own way. But again, let me make this very clear, she doesn't do things her own way in a "Screw you! I'm too cool to conform. Down with The Man!" kind of way. She does things her own way because that is her idea of success. If the rest of the world likes it, then great. And if not, who cares? She is still successful, because *she* has clearly defined success.

Why are you doing what you are doing? Every single day continue to ask yourself, "Why am I in music? What is my idea of success?"

Be specific and honest with yourself. I can't drive it home hard enough: You have *got* to know in detail exactly what it is you want, otherwise you'll drive yourself crazy trying to achieve something when you've not even clearly defined what it is you're trying to achieve.

How do you know whether or not you are successful if you have not detailed your definition of success?

You should not only clearly define success to yourself, but also to those you work with. Trust me on this one, if your idea of success is not traditional or mainstream, don't expect those business people in

Dave Rose (Deep South), Miranda Lambert
City Limits Saloon - Raleigh NC

Miranda has an ear for great songs.
She recorded a song written by Allison Moorer, "Oklahoma Sky."

your life to immediately understand it. Tell them and tell them again. Make sure they understand, and when they do, work with them in helping you achieve those goals.

> *Cousin Rick says:* To date, what would you consider your most successful moment as a musician?

Don't move to L.A.

... Or New York, or Nashville, for that matter. I have met so many bands over the years that have prematurely uprooted from their hometown and moved to Los Angeles, New York, or Nashville. This does not mean you should never move there. Just don't move there yet.

There are great opportunities in music cities like these. It's just easy to get lost in the shuffle, particularly if you've not spent your time honing your skills in your hometown market.

Can you sell out a room of 150 people in your hometown? Have you recorded multiple times with relative success selling your music? Do you have money to sustain yourself for a little while during the time you're getting on your feet in the big city?

The great thing about the music business is that for every rule, there's an exception to that rule. Yes, I'm sure you know many musicians that moved to the big city and ended up successful. My guess is that they would have been successful anyway. It's rare that the move, and the move alone, is the cause for their success. Be careful. Focus on becoming a big fish in your small pond first. You'll start to see doors open when that happens.

> *Cousin Rick says:* Name three great things about the city in which you reside. Every city, even a small one, has something for you to love. List three things.

Q: *Aurelia from Columbia, SC asks: As an independent artist, how can you get a distribution deal with companies such as Target, Wal-Mart, Best Buy, and even Cracker Barrel now?*

A: And you're interested in this, why? When's the last time you went into a brick and mortar store and purchased a CD? If you do regularly, then you're one of the few and sorely out of touch with how people discover new music.

Yes, a few non-traditional outlets are good. Your mention of Cracker Barrel is the best of the four stores you listed. Starbucks probably sells more CDs than Best Buy these days. Still, traditional stores are not how people discover music for the most part.

Don't worry about a distribution deal in stores. They're harder than ever to get, mostly because there are fewer of them, and the ones that are left have smaller and smaller music departments. Why? Because it's not how people buy their music anymore.

Chapter 7:
Social Media

It's not about music, it's about pizza

I was talking with an acclaimed 40-year-old artist recently. This guy has played with some of the greats in the business, performed on the late night talk shows, toured the world and back, and is revered by his peers as a highly skilled musician.

We were discussing social media -- specifically Facebook and Twitter. He shared a sentiment I hear often from musicians predating the Internet generation: "I don't really know what to write about. I don't know what to twit, or twoot, or tweet about, or whatever it's called. And what do I say on my Facebook page? Please 'like' me? I just don't feel comfortable doing this."

He went on to reminisce about coming of age as a musician when he used to hand out flyers for his shows and album releases, the days when he would hit the streets with his staple gun in one hand and a stack of show posters in the other.

Social Media *is* the new flyering.

Deciding what to say on your social media page is no different than the days of passing out flyers. For those of you who remember, or still do it, passing out flyers or hanging posters was something to be done effectively.

Allow me to share one of my early mistakes concerning promotion. After playing my first few shows as a musician to near–empty houses, I had the bright idea to print up flyers. I decided that if I wanted to really pack the place out, I would need to hand out a *lot* of flyers.

So as my next show approached, I printed up nearly 5,000 handbills and flyers. My band and I hit the university campus and quickly passed them out to everyone we saw. Anyone who would take a flyer out of our hands, we would give it to them.

We had done it -- 5,000 flyers passed out at one of the biggest universities in the state. We were sure to be rock stars on the night of the show.

We were positive that of the 5,000 flyers we passed out, at least 500 people that received them would show up.

They didn't. We played to the same 20 friends and family that we always played to.

How could that be? We had covered the campus. I even went back and looked at the flyers thinking I must have put the wrong date on them. But I didn't. The date was right, and it was a professional looking flyer.

I quickly realized that it wasn't about the number of flyers I was passing out, but *how* I was passing them out.

Handing someone a flyer without having a conversation with that person is a waste of time. Just saying, "Here's a flyer to a show," as the person quickly walks by and grabs it out of your hand isn't effective. You may as well be saying, "Here, would you mind throwing this away for me?"

I changed my tactics for the next show. Instead of printing 5,000 flyers I only printed 500. I gave strict instructions to my band that in order to hand out a flyer, we must first have at least a three-minute conversation with the person.

So we headed back out to the same university in preparation for our next show. This time with only 500 flyers in hand, we set out to have actual conversations with 500 people. It took us longer to hand out those 500 flyers with three-minute conversations than it did the 5,000 flyers using our 'shot-gun' method. We told ourselves, "If we don't have a three-minute conversation with a person, we won't hand them a flyer."

It took discipline and time. We all kept feeling the urge to just give a flyer to anyone who would take it. But we resisted and stuck to our plan. Three-minute conversation equals one flyer.

The next show came around. Instead of the same 20 friends and family we had been drawing, we had 110 people who paid at the door.

Five-thousand flyers with no conversations yielded zero results. 500 flyers and real conversations with people yielded an extra 90 people at our show.

Same band. Same venue. Same flyer handed out at the same location. The only difference was that we engaged people in conversation before handing them flyers. We actually asked them about themselves. We asked what kind of music they liked, or where they were from. What's the best place to eat lunch? We talked about anything *they* wanted to talk about. We talked about *them*, not *us*.

As we continued to use this as our method for handing out flyers, we began to make actual friends and fans that would stick by us for years to come. In a world where you couldn't pass through campus without getting handed 15 flyers, we were the ones that wouldn't hand you a flyer unless we got to know you.

Social Media is the new flyering.

Try creating a Facebook event for your band's upcoming show. Then invite 5,000 strangers to the event. I guarantee very few of them will show up.

Then, try to actually interact with 100 strangers on Facebook. Spend time commenting on their page when they post something interesting. Ask them about what they like to do. Talk about similar music or travel interests. Really get to know them in a genuine and friendly way. Then, next time you have a show, invite only those 100 people. Not all of them will attend, of course, but many will if you have genuinely engaged them.

Continue this pattern of creating relationships instead of mass-producing advertisements, and you'll eventually become effective in your own social media network.

Don't wait until you have something to sell or promote to post. Post regularly, but more often than not, post about others -- not about yourself. Post an interesting news story and ask for people's opinions. Personally send messages to some people asking about *their* day, *their* interests, or *their* thoughts on relevant topics. Then, when it comes time for you to promote a show, they will listen.

Back to my conversation with my 40-year-old musician friend who didn't know what to tweet about, or what to write on his Facebook page.

He had posted about shows, or his new releases, and was met with very little response.

So, I said, "Make it about pizza. Everybody loves pizza. Ask people in your network where their favorite places to eat pizza are. Ask them who has the best pizza anywhere in the nation."

And he did.

Typically, this was a guy who would get 5 or 6 comments when he would post something like, "I have a show Friday. Come see me. I'll be at Joe's Bar." But the day he posted, "Who makes the best pizza, anywhere in the nation? What's the best pizza joint?" Dozens and dozens of people responded. He started fun and friendly banter with fans about who actually had the best pizza.

He did this similar type of posting for the next few months. He'd post about almost anything, except himself. He'd ask people's opinions or share a funny story, and he'd engage his network friends in an online conversation about the topic at hand.

When it finally did come time for him to promote a show, he did it with grace, and in a conversational style. It wasn't, "Come see me Friday at Joe's Bar." It was more like, "Friday is the opening of that new Will Ferrell movie. Anybody going to see it? I can't. I'll be at Joe's Bar playing. But if you do go see it, stop by Joe's after and let me know what you thought. But don't tell me how the movie ends!"

In a matter of months he has doubled his crowds at his shows. He made it about *them*, not about him.

Social media isn't about music, it's about pizza. Don't hand out flyers en masse. Ask people where is the best place to get a slice of pizza. Then, after a friendly conversation, give them a flyer. You'll get *far* better results.

> *Cousin Rick says:* Ask your social network friends to tell you their favorite place to eat pizza.

Use social media to engage your current and future fans

Use social media for two primary purposes: to engage your current fan base, and to reach a new audience.

Social media is scary to some because it's so impersonal, but if you treat it like a dialogue, it can be quite enjoyable for the fans. Include them in your creative process. Ask their opinions. Be transparent. Mystery isn't all it's cracked up to be, or used to be. Don't be afraid to share your shortcomings as well as your victories.

Of course you should use social media apps to let your fans know about shows, new releases, and events, but if that's *all* you use it for, they won't hang around long. Get them involved.

Ultimately you will know your music is on the right track when people are telling other people about it, naturally and without prompting. Use social media to monitor this. If you post a new song or video, are people telling their friends?

Let's say you post a new video on Facebook. One hundred of your friends/fans view it but not a single one of them shares it with their friends. If that's the case, then it's pretty safe to say that your music, and video, just didn't move them emotionally enough to spread it around.

Use social media to gauge whether or not your music is moving people. If it's not, get back to the drawing board and write more songs.

In order for you to succeed, your art should move people emotionally. When people are moved, they will tell others naturally. But if your music isn't moving them, no amount of promotion or social media expertise is going to help.

Q: *Taylor from Jackson, MS asks: Can you upload cover songs to sites such as YouTube?*

A: In the time it will take me to write the answer to this, the laws will have likely changed. The laws (and more importantly enforcement of these laws) have been ever evolving in recent years.

The short answer is: Sometimes.

Keep in mind, there's a difference between uploading the original recording of the song, and uploading *your* performance of the song.

Technically, you need a license from the copyright holder to sync picture to music.

It's up to the copyright holder to determine if it's copyright infringement and whether to leave it up or pull it down.

I encourage posting a disclaimer saying that you did not write the song, who did write it, and any other information that may show credit to the artist or composer.

Some copyright holders are more aggressive about removing protected material, while others appreciate the exposure and are more willing to let it slide.

My advice: There are hundreds of articles on the topic online. And like I say, the topic is ever-evolving. So do your homework, not only on the topic, but on the song in question.

Keep in touch

Mystery is certainly becoming a thing of the past with artists. Even those who choose the more mysterious route are up against the challenges of the Internet, where anyone with a cell phone can post pictures and information instantly.

Treat your fans like your friends. Not necessarily like your best friend, who you might tell about your bad case of explosive diarrhea. Not the friend who knows how bad your feet stink, or the friend you'd ask to be the best man in your wedding. Instead, treat your fans like the friend you'd go to a baseball game with, or meet out at the bar for a casual drink from time to time.

Staying in touch with your fans through social media is important. You should draw them in at least once every day. As with anything in your career, maintain a good balance. Don't rely completely on social networking to obtain new fans, but don't ignore it either.

Social media a great way to introduce new people to your music, but nothing can replace the experience of a live show and the passion fans feel when hearing you perform in person. But you've got to let them know you are alive and playing out, so use your social networking sites to keep them updated.

If you do not engage them, you may be traveling eight hours to play a show to an empty room. You would have been better off staying at home and using those eight hours to increase your fan base close to home.

It's more about *how* you use social networking as opposed to *how often*. Engage your fans. If all you're doing is posting, "Hey, I've got a show. Come on out," you're not going to get very good results. Communicate with your social network in ways you would communicate in person. Talk about their interests as much as your own. Over time you'll develop real fans. Fans that know you care about them, and in return they'll care about you

> *Cousin Rick says:* Once a week, share someone else's music with your social network. Then, when you post a new song or video, hopefully others will follow suit and share your music.

Q: *Lauren from New York, NY asks: How often should an artist tweet on Twitter in order to expand a fan base?*

A: It's more about what you tweet than how often. However, you can't go six months without tweeting and expect it to work. My recommendation is at least daily, but on days that are more active, tweet more frequently. If you're on tour, at a performance, or in the studio you should give more regular updates, but make them fun. Engage your audience. Ask their opinions. Get them involved.

At the same time, we don't really care to know when you check your mailbox or feed your cat. Still, on off days, give us something to look forward to, something to talk about, something to make us want more.

My suggestion is make your tweets as much about your fans as about you. Sure, they want to know about you and your music, but ask for their input and you've just strengthened the bond even more.

I've heard a lot of musicians say, "My life is actually kind of boring. I'm not sure what to tweet about."

I won't argue with you there. Most musicians' lives are more humdrum than their fans would probably believe.

So, instead of tweeting, "I'm bored and watching 'I Love Lucy' re-runs," tweet, "My favorite old TV show is 'I Love Lucy'. What's your favorite?"

Instead of tweeting, "Drinking coffee," tweet "Which is better, coffee, tea, or beer? I'm drinking Starbucks now but thinking I may need to switch beverages."

Instead of tweeting, "Going to bed now," tweet, "Going to bed, but putting the tape recorder on the nightstand. I'm feeling inspired to wake up and capture an idea. I'll let you know tomorrow."

Tweet regularly, but not too regularly. One of my favorite quotes is by a famed author who was asked, "How many words should a book have?" He responded with, "Not a single word more than you need." Tweets should be the same. Tweet regularly, but not more than you need.

> *Cousin Rick says:* Right now, send a personal message to a fan whom you have never sent a message. Don't promote something. Ask how they are doing or simply thank them for their support.

YouTube is the new MTV

At one time, MTV was the new radio. The great thing is, anyone can be on YouTube, but tomorrow there will be a new YouTube.

The point is: make a video. People listen with their eyes. Ever since The Beatles appeared on *The Ed Sullivan Show*, people have been fascinated and motivated by seeing their favorite band on TV.

I remember the days when a cheap video was $100,000. Now you can do a video for free. But don't fool yourself into thinking that people want to see you. They don't. People want to be moved. They want to be able to see themselves in your video. They want to see and feel something different. Just because your girlfriend thinks you're hot, don't think the rest of the world cares. It's pointless to make a video unless you really put some creative time and effort into it.

Get others involved. Yes, you can make a video for free, but recruit the help of creative friends. Find an aspiring video editor or director in your area. Likely you can find someone who will be willing to take on the project for free. Getting others involved will perhaps help you to interpret your song in a brand new light. Be open to the ideas of creative people and put together a video that people will want to show their friends, even if they don't know your band.

I've always admired the indie band I Was Totally Destroying It and their ability to get creative videos done locally for very little or no money. They build a good team of creative people around them, and it becomes a fun group project for all involved. Take a moment to research some of their videos online, keeping in mind that most were done for little or no money. (Cousin Rick likes the "Control" and "My Internal Din" videos). You don't have to spend a lot of money to make a great video.

There are millions of videos on the Internet. What's going to set your video apart from the others? You should spend as much time putting together a creative video as you did creating and recording the song itself.

As the world's attention span is getting shorter and shorter, it becomes more and more important to capture attention quickly with a great video.

The Warren Brothers were great at making videos "on the cheap."
You should look this one up: "Sell a Lot of Beer." It's a fun video.

Cousin Rick says: Today, set a date to have your next video completed. Start to make steps each day toward achieving that goal. But set a date: My next video will be released on _____ (MM/DD/YY).

Q: *Gavin from Daytona Beach, FL asks: Should I have a promotional video or MTV style video?*

A: Both. Use your promotional video for the industry: booking, labels, or anyone you're interested in doing business with. Save your professional "MTV style" video for the fans.

Q: *Jasper from Kernersville, NC asks: What is a good setting/background for a promo picture? Do we smile or look like a tough rocker?*

A: I heard a great journalist once say, "Anytime a photographer wants to take your promotional picture outside, beware. What that really means is 'I have this really cool scenic backdrop I'd like to photograph. Maybe I'll stick a band in front of it.'"

Make your promo picture about you, about the band. The setting, scenery, or backgrounds aren't important. Well, they're important only if you screw it up and take a picture on railroad tracks, or in front of the roll-up door to your practice unit. Your promo picture should be about you and your style. If the first thing someone notices when they see your promo picture is the background, then you've taken a bad promo picture.

To smile or not to smile - the age-old question of cool rock bands. My advice is to express the personality of your band in your picture. Is your music dark and mysterious? Then make a picture that reflects that. Is your music happy pop music? Then don't be afraid to crack a friendly smile.

Faking your personality in a promotional picture will be painfully obvious to the viewer. Let your personality, and the personality of your music, be captured in the photo.

Q: *Maria from Portland, OR asks: Is MySpace dead?*
A: Yes.

Chapter 8:
American Idol

If all else fails, audition for American Idol...

If fame is all you're after, auditioning for a TV show might be the way to go. Today, *American Idol*, *The Voice*, and *X-Factor* are the popular shows. Tomorrow it will be something else. But the common thread is the belief in instant fame. Remember though, fortune doesn't always come along for that ride.

Right now, *American Idol* is the most popular show on television. It catapults aspiring singers into instant superstardom. Some go on to achieve pretty decent success. Most do not. But there's a theory that those who do achieve success after the show probably would have achieved it anyway. Who really knows?

Like it or not, *American Idol* is king. It rules the television airwaves. Inevitably, one of the most common questions I get is, "How do I go about getting on American Idol?"

There are auditions throughout the nation leading up to the filming of the show. If you're dead set on going the *American Idol* route, or at least making that one of your options, I'll give you some pointers on how to increase your chances of getting noticed.

For the past several years I have judged the local *American Idol* and *X-Factor* contests that send winners on to direct auditions with the producers.

I'd venture to say I've sat through over 5,000 auditions in the past few years, each singer with the hope and dream of being the next big TV star.

Here are some pointers many of those people auditioning should have read ahead of time:

Me judging the local American Idol auditions.

- Get to the good stuff quickly. Most auditions only give you a minute tops and frequently they cut you before that minute is up. Don't expect to still be around 45 seconds into the song when you get to really wail on that high note. You probably won't be. So get to the good stuff in the first 15 seconds.

- Practice, practice, and practice. Practice with an accompaniment. Practice singing to the real song. Practice in front of the mirror. Video tape yourself singing the song. Your audition will be a capella, so of course practice without music as well.

- Ask several friends if they think you're good enough to audition. Stress that they tell you an honest answer. If you've ever had a friend say, "Yes, those jeans *do* make your butt look big," he or she would be the right person to ask.

- Dress the part. Let the judges know you care about this

audition by looking like you put some effort into your appearance.

- Pick a song that showcases your voice well. Don't do a song that's in the top five on the radio charts. It's likely the judges will be hearing hundreds of others singing that same song. Just do a song that showcases your best attributes.

- The moment before you start singing, consciously remind yourself to take a deep breath. Say something before singing like your name and where you are from. Speaking first will prepare your vocal chords a little, and it will relax you.

- Look at the judges, but don't stare at them. Make regular eye contact with all the judges, but focusing in on one, and perhaps even singing directly to that one judge, rarely works. It may even make the judges uncomfortable.

- Do something that makes the judges remember you. It can be something small. But remember, on that very same day they are hearing you, they are hearing hundreds, possibly thousands, of other singers. Yes, hopefully your voice will be what they remember, but you need more. Perhaps say something after you sing, like, "Thanks for taking the time to listen." At one particular audition, a girl said her name three times before singing and then said, "I just wanted to make sure you remembered my name." We did. Do something small, but memorable.

- Don't wear your Halloween costume or something silly. It's a desperate cry for attention and might be viewed as trying to overcompensate for your lack of vocal abilities. Dress like a star, but don't dress silly.

- Save your voice. You'll need to get to the audition hours and hours before they start. Don't waste your voice talking all morning in line to those around you. Be polite and make some new friends, but don't talk all morning. You will have strained your voice before your big moment.

- Bring a friend. The lines are long and the process of getting in front of the judges can take a lot of time, and possibly give you unnecessary jitters. A friend will help keep you calm and your mind on other things.

- Bring the recording of the song you plan to sing. Load it on your music player and listen to it regularly while standing in line waiting to sing.

- Lastly, millions audition, but only a very few make it. So remember, you need thick skin if you're going down this road. It's unlikely you will make it. Know that in advance. Hope for the best, but don't be disappointed if you get cut. Make the process fun. If you're auditioning in another town or state, make it a fun road trip with a friend. Enjoy the experience, but don't let the rejection get you down.

There are reasons to audition for TV singing shows aside from the experience you gain or the chance that you may actually win. Just getting off your couch and putting yourself out there to audition allows you the opportunity to network with people that you otherwise may have never met. You just might meet other musicians with whom you'd like to stay in contact, or industry professionals who would like to stay in touch with *you*.

One example that comes to mind is a young singer/songwriter named Katie Garfield. I first heard Katie sing when I was judging the preliminary auditions for *X-Factor*. She didn't win, or even get on the show. But *not* winning, even if you're on the show, can prove to be advantageous. That day of the auditions I felt Katie had something special. Her voice was good, but her charisma and integrity shined through even more. From her short audition, I sensed there was something bigger going on, but I couldn't be sure. So I decided to explore further. Soon afterwards, I lined up a meeting with Katie and her parents and we began an informal working relationship where I coached her through the next stages in her career.

I give all the credit to Katie though. On that same day of the auditions I heard another singer -- a guy -- that I really enjoyed as well. Let's call him "Steve." I emailed both Katie and Steve congratulating them on a solid audition. I offered to meet with each. Months later I ran into Steve in line at a coffee shop. He said, *"I'm not sure if you remember me, but you emailed me after I auditioned at X-Factor."*

I said, *"Yes, I remember. You were great. Did you ever email me back?"* (Thinking I may have overlooked the email as I'm sometimes guilty of doing)."

"No. I didn't," he said, slightly ashamed. *"I meant to but I never got around to it."*

"Well, good to see you again, Steve. Enjoy your coffee."

This guy waited in line for 5 hours to audition for *X-Factor* but "never got around" to emailing me back? A task that would have taken only a few minutes? Something tells me the next time I'm in that coffee shop, I'll be buying it from him.

Katie, however, emailed me back immediately to line up a meeting. And if memory serves me, it took me a while to respond, so she emailed me again. Eventually we met. I got her connected with acclaimed songwriter and producer Mike Garrigan who produced her first 3-song demo. Katie has since starred in several TV shows and movies, signed a deal with The Jonas Group, and currently resides in Los Angeles where she is working with some of the top producers and songwriters in the business.

Will Katie Garfield ever become a household name? Only time will tell, but I'm confident she'll do just fine. She is obviously talented but also has a great work ethic. When opportunity knocks, she answers the door.

Auditioning for *X-Factor* and meeting me didn't kick-start her career. Her eagerness to succeed combined with her talent kick-started her career. If it had not been me, someone else would have taken notice of her. And to her credit, she would have been receptive to it, just like she was with me.

It's not enough to just audition. Follow up with anyone and everyone you meet at these auditions. You never know when it may lead to the next step in your career. Auditioning for singing shows can be helpful mostly for reasons that have nothing to do with actually winning the contest.

Katie Garfield on the release day of her first recording.

Cousin Rick says: Go to an audition within the next six months. It doesn't have to be for a singing show. It could be for a local theater show, a singing group, a church musical, or any community audition. It doesn't even need to involve music. But the process of auditioning is something every aspiring musician should do, if for nothing else just for the fun of experiencing something new.

Q: *Sarah from Charleston, SC asks: How do I even get started in the music business? Sounds very basic, but how do you go from playing in your living room/church/school, to actually being a working musician?*

A: *Begin at page one of this book.*

Conclusion

Making music your career is hard. If it were easy everyone would do it.

But realizing *why* it's hard will help you maintain your sanity throughout the process. Primarily it's hard for two reasons: 1) Quite simply, perfecting the art of playing an instrument is hard. It's just not that easy to be great at playing an instrument, singing, or songwriting. 2) There is no guaranteed way to achieve fame or fortune.

If you go to medical school and become one of the greatest minds in medicine, you will very likely make a lot of money and become highly respected in the field of medicine.

If you go to a trade school and learn plumbing, become top in your class and go on to train under some of the great plumbers in your area, it is very likely that you will then become a successful plumber.

That is not the case with music. You can be one of the most brilliant musicians around, and still not make a lot of money or even be recognized as a great musician. Depending on your definition of success, that's not to say you won't succeed. Just becoming a brilliant musician should be reward enough. But if it's money or fame you're after, you will very likely not achieve either in music.

Music is the soul of society. You can't predict or plan what that soul will want. If you happen to be one of the fortunate to feed society's soul with your music, you are to be commended and should be forever grateful. However, very few get that opportunity.

Knowing this very fact will make your journey more enjoyable and realistic. It is very hard to have a career in music because no matter how good you are, it still may not happen.

So enjoy the music. Enjoy the process of making music. Make great music, and then go back and make it better. Have fun with the process. And please, by all means, make a ton of mistakes, just like I did (and still do). The mistakes are half the fun. Don't get all wound up when you make a mistake. Just learn from it, and move on.

You've got to love music if you're going to survive here. Seriously, search deep down and ask yourself that. If you don't *love* music, you should choose another career path.

That's what happened to me. Sure, I love music. No doubt. But more so, I love the marriage of music with money. When my band-mates were busy practicing their instruments or writing songs, I was more interested in making flyers for the next show, or booking the next show, or calling radio stations, or trying to get my band in the newspaper.

One day my drummer said to me, "Do you *ever* practice your bass? It seems like every time I talk to you you're working on promoting the band. You should take some time to practice more." Now that I look back on it, he may have been implying that I wasn't very good at the bass, and I probably wasn't. I wasn't terrible, but I would have been a lot better had I practiced more.

He was right: *if* I wanted to be a professional musician, I needed to live for the music. Instead, I was living to promote the music.

I think we all like the dream, the idea, of being a professional musician. Who wouldn't want to be a rock star? But look deep inside your soul. Do you live, eat, and breathe music? Or are you just starving for attention? As I've said, there are much easier ways to obtain fame or fortune outside of music.

If you live for music, truly live for music, you know it's in your soul. Not fame. Not fortune. The pure joy of music. If that's in your soul, then don't give up. Enjoy the process and make music for the rest of your life. Doing that -- feeding your soul -- will make you successful in music. You still may not have a full time career in music, but you will have been successful.

Stay in touch with me. I made the transition from bass player to music industry guy because I love helping bands and musicians. Send me your stories and your questions. I'm here to help if I can.

You can find me at DaveRose.info or MyCousinRick.com.

I hope you'll stop by to say hello.

Thanks for reading.

Dave Rose

30+ years later and I still haven't changed my hairstyle.

My Cousin Rick

My Cousin Rick